"As a mom who adopted internationally, I found it very interesting to read this account of a different type of adoption: the journey to parenthood via foster care adoption. Ashley did a great job of describing the uncertainty inherent in this type of adoption, as well as the challenges children and parents face as children are settling into a new family. I was rooting for them the entire book and I think other readers will be too."

    MARY OSTYN, blogger at owlhaven.net and r of *Forever Mom: What to Expect ...*

"*Blessed Chaos* is ... a couple's journey through t... story very candidly and with ... on to the children is obvious ... and bad times, reminds us a... r trust in God."

    STACIA WA... ...ᴇɴ, Director, Family Support, Orphan Care Alliance

"Ashley Wells chronicles their journey to parenthood through foster adoption with transparency, humility, and insight. I finished the book in two sittings and only stopped reading because I HAD to go to sleep. Our kids share similar backgrounds and her book shed so much light on what was most likely around the corner for us. This journey can feel really lonely and through this book, Ashley helped me to see that all I was feeling and encountering was normal. I recommend *Blessed Chaos* to anyone adopting through foster care and their support system, such as grandparents and close friends."

    STEPHANIE THOMPSON, mother to 4 children through birth and foster adoption

"Becoming a mom is always an adventure, but Ashley Wells became a mom to four children in an instant. *Blessed Chaos* is Ashley's journey through the foster care system and an adoption process. She authentically shares her story that is packed with joy, doubt, and faith in a way that invites you into her home and heart."

    KRISTIN HILL TAYLOR, author of *Peace in the Process: How Adoption Built My Faith & My Family*

"*Blessed Chaos* is an excellent read for anyone going through or thinking about going through the foster to adopt process. Ashley's honest account of her exciting, often hopeful, often raw journey left me encouraged and validated in my own experiences. As a believer especially, this memoir was a poignant reminder of why we chose to foster. When children are hungry, when they are hurting, when they are scared and neglected; when they need love and I step in and care for them, I am caring for Christ."
> JO MURPHY, mother to 5 children through birth and current foster care placement

"*Blessed Chaos* is a beautiful story that reflects God's heart for uniting Forever Families. Ashley's transparency as she shares her adoption through foster care is sure to bring hope to those walking the same path. Ashley shares the struggles, the joys, the fears, and the faithfulness of God as He made her an instant mother of four. Each and every word of *Blessed Chaos* points to a Savior who desires nothing more than for each of His children to be adopted into His Kingdom forever. A must read for anyone considering adoption or foster care."
> JENNIFER JACKSON LINCK, author of *Bringing Home the Missing Linck: A Journey of Faith to Family*

"*Blessed Chaos* offers a vision of lives living out James 1:27, to take care of the orphans. It displays love in the thick of crisis and loss. This book brought me to tears many times in reliving our foster care experience. It will be very beneficial to foster families all over. Beyond inspiring."
> CHRISTY FARHAR, mother to 7 through birth, fostering and adoption

Blessed CHAOS

A Journey through *Instant* Motherhood

ASHLEY WELLS

Blessed Chaos: A Journey through Instant Motherhood
Copyright © 2014 Ashley Wells

Published by 10:31 Media
www.1031media.com

All rights reserved. No part of this publication may be reproduced in any form or by any means without the prior written permission of the author, except for brief quotations in articles and reviews.

ISBN-13: 978-1503211148
ISBN-10: 1503211142

Cover and author photograph © 2013 Hayley Moss Photography

Scripture quotations are from the ESV® Bible (*The Holy Bible, English Standard Version*®), copyright © 2001 by Crossway, a publishing ministry of Good News Publishers. Used by permission. All rights reserved.

Because of the nature of the internet, any web addresses contained in this book may have changed since publication and may no longer be valid.

It is wise to point out that I am remembering the events portrayed in this book to the best of my ability. I am writing conversations as I remember them. I do know, however, memory can at times be faulty and people may remember different pieces from their own point of view.

This is a true story, but some names have been changed for privacy and security reasons.

Table of Contents

Introduction | *7*
  1 **Our First Day with Four Children** | *11*
  2 **Instant Motherhood** | *25*
  3 **The Chaos of It All** | *41*
  4 **The Blessings Overflow** | *63*
  5 **Family Ties** | *73*
  6 **The Roller Coaster Begins** | *85*
  7 **First Birthdays and the Holidays** | *97*
  8 **The Limbo Life** | *121*
  9 **Final Farewells** | *139*
  10 **The Third Trimester of Foster Adoption** | *153*
  11 **Adoption Day** | *165*
  12 **Life Goes On** | *177*
Afterword | *185*
Resources | *189*
Acknowledgements | *191*
About the Author | *193*

A Journey Worth Sharing
Introduction

"What was it like going from no children to four children in an instant?" I glanced around the restaurant wondering where to start when I was asked this question. I was with some new friends at a much-needed girls' night out. "The first few months went by in a blur," I answered as I began to share my story of motherhood around the table overflowing with delicious Cuban food.

I get asked that question often. It's okay. I don't mind answering. Actually, I love answering. With every answer I get to point, yet again, to God.

The journey to adoption through foster care is not for the faint of heart. In His wonderful goodness He gave me the strength for this journey, even if all I remember is the rapid pace at which it progressed.

Every birth story is miraculous. This is the story of how my family was born. It is miraculous. It is beautiful. It is God's divine plan on display for all to see. I cannot wait as you turn the pages of this book and read about my journey to motherhood and the birth of my family. It was no ordinary birth, although I think that statement may be true for most people. Generally nothing in life happens just as you imagine it would.

I pray as you read my words I will continue to point you back to God, the author of life and the true author of this story. I believe He had always planned for my journey to motherhood to take me along the path it has. In doing so He led me directly to the four children I am blessed to call my sons and daughters. When I was created in my mother's womb, God made my body unable to conceive and carry life within. My children would be born in my heart instead.

This story is not only miraculous because it involves my family being born, but also because every step along the way God led us to where we are now, living life after adoption. I cannot begin to explain, even through the pages of this book, how my entire journey to motherhood has been clearly ordained by God Himself.

My entire life has been guided to bring me to where I am now. Before the creation of the world God, in His goodness, planned for this to come to pass. I know I am living for such a time to have been brought together with my children. How amazing to think of this beautiful truth and know even in the pain and tears there was a great purpose.

A LONG AND BUMPY ROAD

I will start sharing my journey to motherhood in this book around the time we got licensed through our agency. Yet my journey to motherhood started much earlier in my life. During our engagement, Michael and I learned we would likely not be able to conceive. We knew we wanted children, so when the time was right we would explore our options for expanding our family.

In early-2009 we received a clear closed door to even the slightest chance of having biological children. It was a few months later when we decided to start the process of adoption. Making the decision to adopt was just the beginning. Once you make this decision you have to choose where you want to adopt from, what agency you are going to use, what your restrictions will be for placements, and much more. It is a daunting process, but so worth the end result.

We were licensed in Ohio before we moved to Kentucky in 2010, but we never received a phone call for placement. We were licensed at that time for up to two children aged six and younger whose biological parents already had their rights terminated. This was a "safer" route in our mind. Once we moved to Kentucky, we decided to start the process again and open up some of our restrictions. The Lord had been working in us and gave Michael and I the courage to risk the safety of our hearts. Although our time waiting in Ohio was extremely painful, I see now the reason we never got a phone call. Our kids weren't there. They were waiting for us in Kentucky.

Whatever you may be going through right now, don't lose hope! You never know what is ahead of you. The waiting is never easy, but it is often necessary. We have to trust and be confident of the fact the Lord is in control. Our hardships are often the places where God chooses to grow us the most.

I am learning to see my difficult seasons through the perspective the Bible offers in James 1:2-4, "Count it all joy, my brothers, when you meet trials of various kinds, for you know that the testing of your faith produces steadfastness. And let steadfastness have its full effect, that you may be perfect and complete, lacking in nothing." There is a purpose for everything we face on this earth.

God has a plan for our lives and His plans are so good. We only get to see a glimpse of the big picture on this side of Heaven, yet we can hold tight to our faith and know everything will work together for our ultimate good. Eventually, the long and bumpy road of our trials will end and we will be a living testimony to God's faithfulness and sovereignty in the lives of His children.

Our First Day with Four Children
Chapter One

I will never forget the moment I saw my children for the first time. I had walked into our agency in April of 2012 with a different purpose than in the past. I wasn't turning in paperwork or completing a training. I was going to bring home children.

I walked through several doors and into a holding area where I stood staring out the windows and waiting. I watched for a car to pull up and four children to be unloaded and brought inside to meet me. This was an emergency placement. Michael and I had no idea what the future would hold with these children.

Let's step back a moment. When Michael and I were licensed through our agency, we had told them we only wanted to be called for children who were nearing adoption. We didn't want to walk the tight rope of fostering for long before being able to legally welcome children into our family. We believed our hearts were too fragile from the journey through infertility to risk any more uncertainty on the road to parenthood. I have to laugh as I type that now. This safe reality was not God's plan for our family.

I remember praying in the depths of my hurt through Ephesians 3:20, "Lord, I am hurting. Yet I know Your Word says You are able to do far more abundantly than all we ask or think. You know my heart to be a mother, Lord. I pray You would bring our children to us. I can't even imagine the goodness You have planned for my life. Whether our journey to parenthood is through birth or adoption, make it clear to us Lord Jesus. I cannot wait to see the marvelous plans You have for us. Lord, may You work according to Your great power within us and be given the glory forever and ever. Amen." I knew He was going to move mountains one day to make me a mother.

The phone call on April 24th wasn't at all what we were expecting. There were four children: Jonathan, an eight-year-old boy; Jazmine, a five-year-old girl; Christina, a thirteen-month-old girl; and Kyle, a two-and-a-half-week-old boy. *Oy!* We had said we were willing to accept up to four children aged eight-years-old and younger. The Lord surprised us and brought into our lives just that!

The children had been removed from their biological parents' care that day and we were their first foster care placement. Suddenly, we found ourselves right at the beginning of the process of them being in foster care and we had no idea how long the children would be with us or if we would ever get the chance to adopt them into our family. It was scary to look ahead and not know what would happen.

THE PHONE CALL THAT CHANGED EVERYTHING

It was mid-afternoon on the 24th of April and I was on the phone with one of my best friends, Maegan, who lived in Washington State. I was cuddled up on our coach under a blanket and felt drained.

"My heart is so weary from all this waiting," I confessed to Maegan.

It was Tuesday, and we had just been licensed on the previous Thursday. We had a respite placement that weekend and the children had gone home the day before. (A respite placement is when foster parents temporarily care for foster children that are placed in a different home to give the current foster parents relief or because an emergency has occurred. These are temporary placements.) Having children in our home, even just temporarily, had been incredibly refreshing.

We had a cookout with the three children from the respite placement and had played in the backyard for hours watching as these children had what seemed to be unending energy. I was sad to see them go, although we knew from the beginning they were only staying for the weekend. I still cried most of the car ride home after dropping them off, though. It had been glorious to simply get a taste of what being a mother was like. I was crying out for God to bring home my kids.

At this point, we were waiting for a phone call that would bring a more long-term placement into our lives; a placement that would hopefully end in adoption. Honestly, though, I was weary from all the waiting.

I was mid-sentence with Maegan, "I just want my kids (beep beep) to come home." I looked at the screen of the phone and saw our agency was on the other line. My stomach immediately jumped within me. I told Maegan I had to call her back and I quickly answered the new call. They had a placement for us!

I heard the placement details and my heart physically hurt in my chest so much I placed my hand there as if reciting the Pledge of Allegiance. With each new word I was struggling to breathe. I knew in that instant if we said yes it would be a long and dangerous road to the end, if we even got there. Michael was at work so I requested a few minutes to get in contact with him before accepting the placement. The worker stressed needing to know our answer quickly because these kids had nowhere to go.

I had no idea what we were going to do. Did I want to say yes? *Of course!* Was I terrified of what an affirmative answer would mean for us and what our future would be? *Beyond a doubt.*

As I dialed Michael's work number with shaking fingers and on the verge of tears I prayed, "Lord, help him to know what to say. Guide him with peace." The phone rang. No answer. I called again. No answer. I called Maegan back and told her what was happening. Then Michael called in on the other line. Maegan said she would pray for us and then I switched over to talk to Michael.

"They have a potential placement for us," I said with trepidation. As I told Michael the details, he was quiet. I asked him what he wanted me to tell our agency worker. *"Yes!"* He said that three-letter-word as if there was no other real option. The tears began to run down my face and suddenly I knew too. Michael continued with confidence in his voice, "These could be OUR children. We can't NOT say yes."

After that statement I began sobbing, and for that matter I cry as I type these words and remember the beauty of this moment of faith. I'm so thankful the Lord gave Michael the words to say in one of our most-urgent life-altering moments. We knew we would have to make monumental decisions in a matter of moments and had prayed for exactly that moment during the years leading up to this decision.

"Lord give us peace to know exactly what to do when we are called about placements," had been a spoken prayer between

Michael and me most nights before we went to sleep. Praise the Lord for answering our prayers through Michael.

I ended the phone call with Michael and began the journey to that holding room a mere ninety minutes later, standing in front of a window, waiting to lay eyes on these four children for the first time.

I stood at those windows in the holding room with butterflies dancing in my stomach. It felt like I would burst into tears, or start shaking, or throw up at any moment. Maybe all three, who knows? There were lots of emotions in those moments of waiting. I was intentionally focusing on my breathing, trying to calm myself down. I could have used a brown paper bag to breathe into.

Those moments found me praying. *"Lord, give me the courage to love these children with all I have even though I don't know if I will get to adopt them one day."* Despite knowing whether these children would be mine to love forever, I wanted to love them with everything in me for as long as I had the chance. They deserved to be loved like that. Every child does.

The receptionist must have sensed my nerves and so she gently got my attention and asked if there was anything she could help me with. I answered, "I'm just waiting for a foster care placement. They should be here any minute. It's our first placement."

She smiled wide and bright then asked for more details. It was the first time I got to tell someone, in person, we were finally going to be parents, going from having no children to four children. This was also the first of many shocked and surprised responses I would get. I let out a nervous laugh, trying not to pass out from the overflow of emotions, and then went back to my spot in front of the window.

SEEING THE KIDS FOR THE FIRST TIME

With each car that drove by I felt a rush of excitement. *Could this be them?* I saw a woman, the state investigative worker, get out of the driver side and start unloading kids; I saw a boy, a girl, then a toddler, and a car seat. It was them! I held back tears as I watched them come toward the building. I had to fold my hands in front of me because they had started to shake. I didn't want to scare the kids, they were supposed to feel safe coming home with me. I couldn't look like the emotional mess I felt.

I walked toward the main door to greet them into the holding room. As I opened the door, and was moments away from meeting them, the receptionist asked, "Are those your kids?" I smiled and felt a temporary sense of peace rush over me as I replied, "Yes, I do believe they are." There were so many thoughts running through my mind in those seconds as we prepared to meet for the first time, *"Am I going to adopt these children one day? Oh my word, they are beautiful. I am taking these kids home. I am taking these kids home! What have I gotten myself into?"*

I stared at their faces as they finally walked through the main doors and started toward me. It was as if I was checking in the delivery room for ten fingers and ten toes. I was seeing these children for the first time and then I would be taking them home as mine, at least temporarily. I saw Jazmine's bright red hair. I looked at Jonathan and noticed how tall he was. Christina was crying and so confused. Kyle was the smallest baby I would ever hold, up until that point in my life, at only six pounds and a few ounces. He was sleeping in those first moments though, so I had to admire him from afar.

Our agency worker, Tim, joined us moments later and we started going through lots of paperwork while I also tried to watch the kids explore the holding room full of toys. Instead of an experience, it was more a process. I was signing papers one right after another and we were talking about how I would need to enroll Jonathan in school, if I wanted to put Jazmine in preschool, and how we were going to have the bedrooms set up. All the while there was a thirteen-month-old crawling around the floor crying and searching for something, anything, familiar while the big kids started ripping toys off of the shelves and finding distractions from the boring grown-up talk.

The kids were hungry, having not had anything to eat yet that day (and it was after six o'clock in the evening). The same receptionist who I talked with before found them some snacks and they ate like they had hardly eaten anything their whole lives. I would later find out this was quite true and was only just a beginning glimpse of the neglect they had encountered in their short time on this earth.

My paperwork was finally done and there was now copying and paperwork for the workers to sign. I started a game of *Hi Ho Cherry-O* with the big kids when unexpectedly Christina wanted to play and all the cherries were abruptly on the floor.

My first motherhood moment of chaos happened in that holding room. I remember a few staff members who had been watching us and were now laughing innocently as I tried to keep Christina from eating one of those little red plastic cherries while cleaning them up and explaining to the big kids why it probably wasn't the best time to play that particular game.

Around the same time, Kyle woke up and I held him for the first time. I was in complete awe of this tiny little man, even with the chaos around me. I realized as I stared down at his eyes, which were looking up at me, how amazingly blessed I was to have the privilege to care for these children, no matter how long. My eyes began to water and I had to find something to distract myself before the floodgates opened.

Michael and I had never imagined we would get the

opportunity to care for an infant, and we were okay with it. We knew the Lord had plans for us and we had thought they were for us to adopt older children. Yet now with Christina and Kyle it was as if the Lord not only gave us this unexpected opportunity, which we weren't expecting, but doubly blessed us. It was one of the most surprising aspects of this journey: being able to experience the beauty of the newborn stage at least once.

WELCOME HOME

The paperwork was done, the investigative state worker left, and our agency worker, Tim, helped me load the kids into our minivan with nothing more than a blanket on top of Kyle, a can of formula, a box of diapers, and the clothes on each of their backs. I spent the car ride home asking the big kids about themselves and then telling them about Michael and I and what to expect at our house, like our three cats and the room arrangements.

Jonathan asked me to explain the bed arrangements a second time. He questioned, "I'll have a room and bed all to myself?" He appeared struck by the fact he was going to have a bed just for him. My heart broke a little more at this realization.

These children had been living about thirty minutes away from our home and had up until this point been living in circumstances I could not even begin to imagine, but would learn more about slowly over the following months. I knew children in America were living in poverty and less-than-ideal situations, yet I don't think I had ever taken the time to slow down and truly think about the desperate lives children were living within miles of where I lay each night warm and with a full stomach of food.

Michael was home from work when we pulled up to our house and he had made dinner for us all. He opened the door wide and greeted us with such a joyful face, it was as if seeing a memory from our wedding day when he first got a glimpse of me walking down the aisle toward him. As Michael held the door open, the kids walked in first. I followed and entered our home for the first time proudly with full hands, holding Christina in one arm and Kyle's car seat carried by the other. Michael smiled knowingly at me as he glanced around at our now-full house with watery eyes.

We made dinner plates quickly and set the three big kids up at the table, Kyle had fallen back asleep in the ride home and was still slumbering quietly. While the kids were devouring, *ahem*, I mean eating their chicken tacos, we quickly realized we didn't have any pajamas or clean undergarments for the kids.

After eating, Michael and Jonathan left for the store to get necessities we needed to get through the night. Once the girls were all done with their first meal with us, I got them into the bathtub to get cleaned up. Kyle was still sleeping at this point and I breathed in a moment of ordinary, beautiful motherhood: bath time with two gorgeous giggly girls.

While I watched the girls in the bath I took the time to reply and call people back since having shared our news. I made sure everyone knew we didn't know anything about our future with the kids or how long they would be with us. Michael and I knew we were risking the safety of our hearts with this placement, but we weren't sure if everyone else would be able to do the same and we were certain to make it abundantly clear this was not an adoptive placement, yet.

Michael and Jonathan came home after a little while and everyone got into their new pajamas. Bedtime is difficult for most children, but this bedtime was a nightmare. The kids had just experienced a whirlwind kind of day and had no idea what was happening. Christina screamed as she tried to go to sleep. Jazmine was crying and begging for her mommy and daddy. Jonathan was crying and seemed confused as well, but also simply seemed tired. It took lots of reassuring words and pats on the back to calm them down. Then, one by one the kids settled and drifted off to sleep.

Michael and I washed dishes together after the kids were in bed and spoke amazed and terrified at the same time, we wondered what was ahead for us. *Were we really ready? Could we handle the emotional turmoil that would surely come? Could we handle parenting four kids?*

Our first day was coming to a close.

Well, not really.

We had a newborn who hadn't consistently been fed. Therefore, he woke us up every hour eating about an ounce of formula (probably just checking to see if the food was still going to be there). Michael and I were high on adrenaline though, so we didn't mind it too much. We did try to get as much sleep as we could though, knowing we were entering unfamiliar territory and had no idea what the coming days, weeks, and months would hold.

As I woke up around the sixth time that first night, I held Kyle comfortably as he took his bottle. Despite being exhausted already, I knew God was doing something amazing in each moment with these children. I remember praising the Lord in those wee-morning hours for bringing these children into our lives and asking for the strength to persevere on the journey.

Instant Motherhood
Chapter Two

The next day Michael and I woke up very early, no need for an alarm! The children had never been in a routine and didn't know natural cues (like the sun rising) to help them wake up. We were up far earlier than we were used to and before the sun. The kids were awake and hungry though, so the day needed to begin (even though I'd much rather have been asleep in my bed exhausted from the night waking up with Kyle).

The kids and I had much to get done and Michael had to work. Therefore, it was my first full day as a mom and on top of that I was going to be alone with four children I had just met and a list of things we needed to get accomplished. Looking back I am surprised at how much confidence I had in this task. We ate breakfast and got busy tackling our list of things we had to do.

First we had to go to our residing elementary school and see if we could get Jonathan into a second grade class there. Unfortunately, it was full so we had to apply to other schools that were close to us. The added process gave us a couple extra days with Jonathan before he went to school, which I am thankful for in hindsight. This delay gave us time to get to know him more and him get to know us before having to send him to school each day.

After visiting the school, we needed to run to the store and get toothbrushes and other necessities we had forgot about in the first night's run for pajamas and underwear. This shopping trip also included getting more clothes for each child since they were wearing the same clothes I had washed from the previous day.

Moreover, we would need more food. Our weekly shopping trip for Michael and I would not last long since we had more mouths to feed. Thankfully, I didn't have to worry about dinners. Our church and other friends blessed us abundantly with dinners for the first month we had the kids. Many times the meals were large enough to have leftovers for lunch as well. Providing us meals was one of the foremost ways in the beginning of this process in which we felt cared for by our Louisville friends.

I remember walking in the health and beauty aisles searching for the children's toothbrushes when my mom called me to ask how we were doing. She was three hours away and wishing she could be with me. It made my heart so happy to see her right from the beginning open her heart to these precious children.

Kyle started crying and the big kids were getting a little rowdy. "Hold on, Mom," I said as I sat the phone on a shelf next to the toothbrushes as I attempted to settle down my crew.

When I picked the phone back up, with Kyle now in my arms, I remember her asking me where I was. I replied saying we were at the store picking up a few things. She then said, in complete seriousness, "What?!? You are out by yourself with all the kids?"

"Yes Mom," I replied. "How would I get anything done if I stayed home all day?" She asked how I was doing it, like logistically. I laughed at the question. With just my sister and me, she couldn't imagine how I was surviving with four kids, let alone going out in public alone with them. She proceeded to get off of the phone with me, rather abruptly, so I could focus on the task at hand.

My mom's words of unbelief would be the first of many comments I would receive about our family size and managing. I hadn't realized four children would cause us to stick out in public. Even still, we hardly go anywhere without remarks of "having our hands full." I always reply with a smile, "Yes, we are very blessed." Which is exactly how I feel.

Many people can't imagine having four children, let alone becoming a mother to all four in different stages of life in an instant. It wasn't easy, but yet I know the Lord had prepared me for such a time as this. As I heard by Michele Cushatt on a podcast recently, "Just because something is hard, doesn't mean it's not good. And just because something is hard, doesn't mean you're not called to it."[1]

I knew, even in the chaos, this is what I was called to do. It didn't make managing life any easier, but I confidently trusted in the truth I was there, with Michael and these four children, in those moments for a purpose, destined and called by God. Life isn't always easy, but it doesn't mean you aren't exactly where you are supposed to be.

THE BEGINNING BUSYNESS

Just a few days after the kids came to us, we had to take them to the doctor for their first examinations. They were able to see all the kids at once, which was supposed to save us time and energy. In the moment, though, it was not the best three hours of our lives. *Yes. Three hours. In one exam room. With all six of us, Michael included.*

One by one the kids were examined thoroughly, given TB tests, and then we had to schedule ongoing appointments to get their vaccinations up to date and stay current with their well-child visits. *Who knew you had to visit the doctor so much when*

---

[1] Lipp, Kathi (Host). #108: Following God isn't Always Pretty - with Michele Chushatt. *So Here's the Thing with Kathi Lipp* [Audio Podcast]. Retrieved from http://www.kathilipp.com/podcast/.

children are little? Not me. We would be at the doctor on average twice a month for the first year.

In those first hours at the doctor we learned of the children's direct exposure to drugs and alcohol, not only observing but participating. It was eye opening to the depth of neglect and lack of supervision they had lived through, and survived, nearly the entirety of their lives up to this point. Jazmine and Jonathan shared with the doctor how they had been invited to try a variety of drugs and alcohol, and also how Christina would often discover half empty bottles of beer that she would drink.

While at the doctor we also spoke about the children's appetites, which had continued to be quite ferocious. The doctor helped us with some tips to teach the kids we would always have food and understand they didn't have to overeat at each meal for fear of how long they would have to wait to be fed again. It had become a habit of survival.

For some kids, it helps for food to be displayed, like fruits and snacks, so they know and see there will always be food. For our kids, however, when they saw food they felt like they had to eat it. All of it. Because of this, we couldn't keep food out and visible on the counter. The doctor also suggested not bringing the serving dishes to the table at meal times, but keeping them out of sight so the kids weren't tempted to ask for more just because they saw more.

That first week with the kids we also had our first home visit with our agency worker, Tim. These visits would occur weekly for the first month and then continue monthly. Tim was always supportive and pointed us to resources that would help us continue to adjust well. Not only that but he was a fountain of wisdom and information.

We would later be assigned a different worker, Angela, who was also helpful and would see us through to the end. However, Tim was perfect for our introductory months because of his knowledge, perspective, and experience. He was an asset as we adjusted to this new life and he remained available to us throughout the entire process when needed.

We hadn't thought much about the increase of appointments and overall busyness that would come from adding four foster children to our family. *Whew!* It was a lot. With school drop-offs and pick-ups, doctor appointments, home visits, and more things being added, life started moving at a rapid pace.

FALLING IN LOVE

Nights were still hard and crying was a guarantee. That first week was so tiring. I didn't sleep more than ninety minutes at a time. I am amazed at how the Lord sustained us and gave us strength to press on each day and each moment. I remember feeling unbelievably exhausted, yet I was able to get through whatever obstacle I faced. As soon as Michael or I would find ourselves with feelings of not possibly being able to do anything else, strength would come and we would do what needed done.

Isaiah 40:28-29 says, "Have you not known? Have you not heard? The LORD is the everlasting God, the Creator of the ends of the earth. He does not faint or grow weary; his understanding is unsearchable. He gives power to the faint, and to him who has no might he increases strength." God giving us the power to get through each day is the only explanation for how we made it. By His power, He gave us strength when we were faint and weary. Even when we felt like we couldn't take one more step, we would move forward in faith and be sustained.

We discovered the children had been told, in the last moments with their biological parents, they would be returning home or living with their grandma very soon. It was on the fourth day with us Jazmine and Jonathan realized this probably wasn't true. It was as if we were soothing them on the first night all over again.

The nights were incredibly difficult. Many times there was just inconsolable crying until they would fall asleep. In those moments I would do the only thing I could think: hold them, rock them, pat their backs, sing lullabies, and pray over them. I wanted to do anything to make them feel safe.

On that fourth night I was tired, bone weary. It was a struggle to even walk from room to room. I put each kid to bed and soothed their worries one by one until they were asleep. Christina was always first because she was the most difficult, and no one else could possibly go to sleep while she was still screaming. Once she finally closed her eyes I moved my attention to the top bunk where Jazmine had begun resting with a few books. Wiping tears away I gave her a hug, read her a story, said a prayer, sang a quiet song, and then finally I patted her on the back. She was a little bit easier.

Jonathan was next. He and Michael had been spending time together, with Kyle close by, as I got the girls asleep. Now it was his turn. He was ready and simply rested after a prayer. Kyle was the last one, the easiest of the four. As I held him and watched him enjoy his bottle, tears started to come. I couldn't hold them back any more. I hadn't cried yet. I was still holding it all in since meeting the kids. I let out all the built-up emotions from the week. I watched Kyle, so precious and comforted by my embrace. I was in awe of these kids and this life. I was in love. I was so happy. It was so hard. Yet I was doing it, thanks to God. In those moments I cried out of desperation and exhaustion, yet also amazement. Then fearful tears started to fall down my face fast and heavy.

I was already terrified. *What if they left? What if I had to say goodbye?* My heart would already be broken, and it hadn't even been a week. I couldn't believe how I had already fallen in love with these children, despite any biological relation.

You wonder sometimes as you are preparing to adopt, will you truly love these children even though you share no DNA? Let me tell you: Yes. I was already absolutely undeniably in love with each of the children. *What if they were with us for months and then go back to their biological parents? What then? How would I go on knowing what my life could be like?* Now that I had experienced these precious moments with children, I didn't want to go on without these kids.

I cried and cried and cried, wiping my tears away with the burp cloth as I held Kyle and watched him take his bottle and softly fall asleep. I was so overwhelmed with emotion. Love. Fear. Awe. Excitement. Exhaustion. It was all too much.

Michael saw me crying and asked me what was wrong. All I could mutter out through the tears was, "I'm already in love." Michael joined me in our room where I put Kyle to bed with tears continuing to stroll down my face. Michael held me as we stared at Kyle drifting off to sleep and I cried a puddle of tears on my pillow. That night we enjoyed six hours of uninterrupted sleep and woke feeling new and ready to face the world again.

FAMILY AND OPEN HEARTS

When the kids came to us they had no clothes but what was on their backs. I had picked up a couple outfits on our first trip to the store and we would soon be receiving vouchers which allow for children new to the foster care system to receive an extra one-time stipend to get clothes and shoes when they first come into care. Little did I know, when my mom had called me at the store checking in on everyone she had other plans. I hadn't thought much of the fact she had asked for sizes. Yet when my sister Andrea (who also lived three hours away) showed up at our house with bags full of clothes and shoes and toys for the kids I knew they had conspired together to serve us and bless the children.

Not only that, but Andrea stayed for several days. She helped with manpower and also loved on the kids and did things around the house for us. That weekend she was acting weird and I knew she was hiding something. I questioned her, "What are you hiding?" That's all it took, she couldn't hold it in any longer. She then shared that within the hour my mom and two of my aunts were going to be arriving for a surprise visit.

Sure enough, my aunt's van pulled up and out came my mom and aunts and a few cousins even. Not only did they surprise us with their presence, but they had each (along with Andrea) chosen one of the kids and brought things for them: even more clothes, toys, shoes, and more. Plus they brought lots of food.

All of us women sat around our patio table in the backyard after dinner watching the children run around and play. I made sure they knew we had no idea how long the kids would be with us. They replied, "They are here now. That's all that matters."

I was overwhelmed at their love and generosity. This is the same kind of reaction we received from so many people who stopped by to say hello, or wanted to bring something for the children, or brought us dinner. We were amazed as we witnessed people who were willing to open their hearts to these four children, even considering the risk that they might return to their biological family.

The kids were over the moon with each visit. Later I would come to understand that for most of their lives they were just pushed to the side as other things appeared to be of greater importance. Yet day after day we had visitors whose sole purpose was to bless the children and let them know they were loved and wanted. I remember Jonathan asking me one day as we were eating a dinner brought by a family in our church, "Why do all these people care so much about us?" With tears forming in my eyes, I placed my hands on his shoulders, staring directly at him, and replied, "They care about you because we have been praying for many years for God to bring us children to love. And look! He has brought us you! We are so happy to take care of you and love you for as long as you need us!" He smiled back at me and then wrapped his arms tight around me.

I remember many times answering questions like this from Jonathan. From the beginning he was surprised to know we wanted them at our house. It was as if in his mind he couldn't imagine being wanted somewhere instead of just being there or taking up space or being in the way. I remember time and time again he would just come up to me and hug me saying, "Thanks for taking care of us." Or "Thank you for feeding us again."

CHILDREN WILL BE CHILDREN

To say we jumped into parenting head-first would be an understatement. It was more like standing under one of those huge buckets of water at an indoor waterpark that dumps onto the people below after being filled up with a massive amount of water. You can hardly keep your bathing suit up when the water crashes onto you. In a much similar way, we were welcomed into parenting with four children at all different stages of life.

Kyle, the newborn, was the easiest to adjust to. He mostly slept and ate during those first few weeks. Michael and I would hold him as he took his bottle throughout the day and night. It was easy to bond with him, he didn't resist. He accepted our loving care willingly and reciprocated with smiles and cooing.

Christina, at thirteen-months-old, was already in the throes of toddlerhood it seemed. She threw loud screaming fits frequently throughout the day and would accompany those fits with thrashing movements on the ground. She also didn't like to be held or accept cuddles. She had become independent, out of necessity, and did not accept correction or assistance in completing tasks very well. Because of this, Christina was often a difficult child. It was a struggle to bond because I hardly had positive moments with her between her fits and lack of touch.

Jazmine was five-years-old and still in a stage of throwing uncontrollable temper tantrums when she didn't get her way. It only took a couple of days for the first one to occur. Then they began to take place several times throughout the day and would at times be disruptive and involve hitting and kicking walls and screaming how she did not like us, or thought we were mean, or didn't want to be at our house.

Jonathan, eight-years-old, lasted much longer without any behavior problems. Disrespect and anger began to show themselves occasionally in his behavior. At this point, though, he would general stomp away to his room and shut the door when receiving correction, or simply accept it.

I quickly reserved some parenting books from the library and also took advice from Tim, our agency worker, at home visits. I needed some parenting strategies quick. One of the main sources of conflict were sibling arguments, especially between Jazmine and Jonathan. We realized they didn't know how to play well together or show kindness to each other when struggles came. Later this would become one of the first things we worked on in family therapy.

BEING A NEW MOM (TIMES FOUR)

I see many new moms with their cute little babies, sitting around talking about which cloth diapers to use, or which bottles are best, or paying lots of money for beautiful cute clothes, or taking lots of pictures and sharing every milestone on Facebook. I think this is pretty common for first-time moms.

Here's the thing: I was a first-time mom, but to four children. I didn't experience motherhood in the same way most people do. I was an instant mom. I couldn't worry about some of the smaller issues for Kyle because I had three other children I was learning about and taking care of. I couldn't focus too much on taking pictures in the first few months, because as soon as I would pick up my camera a toddler would be trying to climb up the refrigerator or ride a cat like a horse or something of similar urgency and my focus would get shifted.

In some ways I am sad I didn't get the normal introduction to motherhood. I didn't get to just enjoy Kyle in all his newborn-ness and cuddle him all the time. Nor did I get that experience with my other three children. Christina didn't like to be held and the big kids were distant at first. I am sad about that. I missed so much of their lives.

Looking back now, I wish I would have had the time to hold Kyle more. I wish I could have been sure to look Christina in the eyes and make her laugh every day, experience those happy moments together. I wish I would have remembered to slow down and give Jazmine and Jonathan more hugs and kisses, despite how old they were.

I see families with these photo albums of everything in their child's life. We simply don't have that. We don't have shared memories from infanthood on with all of our children. And honestly, I'm not sure if any of us will really remember those first few months together in the haze of chaos. I'm sure I missed countless opportunities for small, but meaningful moments in the mess of it all. We were all doing the best we could.

Adoption isn't for the faint of heart. At times, especially in the beginning, I craved a normal introduction to motherhood. Kyle was easy to bond with, I wanted it to not be so hard with the other children too. On especially difficult days I wondered why the Lord had led me to this path. *Why couldn't it have been easier? Why couldn't I have just given birth to children? Why did it have to be so hard?*

I know God didn't call us to an easy life on this earth, Jesus actually guaranteed to His disciplines in John 16:33 they would have trouble. In the same breath He gave them hope though, "But take heart; I have overcome the world." He also gave the promise of peace to be found in Him just previous to the guarantee for trouble. If anything, my questions and struggles were an indicator I was living right where I should be, right where God wanted me.

I could focus on the sadness of this quick head-first jump into motherhood, or I could try to embrace it.

You see, I didn't have time to focus on some things of lesser importance because I had too much else to focus on. The minute I would start to focus on something somewhat trivial to my daily motherhood task, I would be reminded I had to be present most every moment of the day because someone would need me or be getting into something and need parental intervention. That is the great advantage of this kind of sudden introduction to motherhood: I only had the time to focus on the things that mattered in the day-to-day care of the children.

The Chaos of It All
Chapter Three

"The state investigative worker just called and arranged a visitation with Aaron for tonight," Tim made this unexpected phone call a week after the kids had been with us. It was completely out of the blue. Michael and I had no idea what was going on, and received no warning. We were under the impression Madison and Aaron, the kid's biological parents, would have to do a few things before they'd be allowed to see the kids. Tim didn't have any answers to our questions on how a visit could occur so soon, he simply knew one was happening and we needed to be there. He made it clear, our investigative state worker had set the visitation and we had to comply despite our questions. I was hoping all day long we would get a phone call canceling the visit, yet it never came. We ate an early dinner after school and loaded everyone into the van.

We used the drive to the agency to tell the kids they were going to get to visit with Aaron, the three younger children's biological father. Jazmine and Jonathan seemed excited for the visit, especially Jazmine who was confirming with squeals of delight, "What? I'm going to see my dad?" Jonathan immediately asked, "Why isn't my mom going to be there too?" We were told Madison had checked into a rehabilitation center. We told the children she was at the doctor getting help so she could be healthy for them.

They continued to have many questions about what was going to happen exactly. *How long will we see him? Will you be there? Does this mean we get to go home?* We told them, "You are all still coming back home with us, this is just a visit. But it's really exciting and we hope you have fun seeing your dad!"

Despite my concerns, I wanted to be an encouraging voice in the children's lives. I never wanted to bad-mouth Madison or Aaron to the children, instead I always sought to give them the respect they deserved as the children's biological parents. We could never take away the connection they had.

This was our first visit too, so we weren't sure how to prepare the kids since we didn't know what to expect either. I was worried and had an upset stomach since hearing of the visit, I hadn't been able to eat and felt nauseous. I wondered what type of reaction we would get from Aaron. *Would he resent us for taking care of the kids? Would he be supportive of our role in the children's care? Would he arrive in a good frame of mind to interact with the kids? Would he say anything inappropriate to them?*

We arrived at our agency a few minutes early and caught up with Tim. He told us the visit was set for only an hour and it would end at the time set whether Aaron arrived on time. We waited and waited. The big kids stood at the same window I stood at just a week earlier. They were watching for a car to pull up and their biological father to come walking toward us. The irony of this moment sat heavy on my chest. I held Kyle and fed him while we were all restless wondering what was to come.

The visit time was halfway over and there was still no sign of Aaron. The room was getting busier with other visits going on as well. We were trying to keep the big kids distracted to make the time go by, but they didn't want to leave their spot at the window. With twenty-five minutes still to go, Aaron arrived and was greeted with joyful screams from Jazmine. Michael and I were briefly introduced to him, shook hands, and then were escorted out of the room. It all happened fast.

Michael and I sat in chairs outside of the holding room with a heavy reminder that nothing was a guarantee in this process to adopt from foster care. Madison and Aaron were the children's biological parents and they would, rightfully, be given much time and many opportunities to repair what was broken in their lives and get their children back. If they were unable to do what was necessary to provide a safe and healthy living environment for the children, we would then be at the mercy of the state and our judge. It was a jolting realization that shook us back to reality as we held hands and waited for the visit to end.

Twenty-five minutes never felt so long, but finally Tim came to us again and said it was time for the visit to end. As we entered back into the holding room I noticed Jazmine gripping Aaron's arm tighter the closer I walked toward them. For her, I was a reminder this visit was just a short and temporary occurrence. She didn't want the visit to end. Kyle was put in my arms and I buckled him into his car seat. Christina was hugged goodbye and started screaming as Michael picked her up. He held Christina and the car seat and told the big kids it was time to go. Jonathan said goodbye and started crying while walking away with Michael. I still remember having to pull Jazmine away while she was crying and screaming and trying to reach out of my grip and return to her daddy.

We loaded the children in the van, each one accompanied with wet faces from the tears pouring out of their eyes. We tried to remain as calm as we could so we could reassure them everything was okay. It didn't matter what we did, though, they did not feel like everything was okay. They were being ripped away again from a familiar face, the only one they had seen in the past week. I'm sure seeing Aaron was a reminder of the fact they had lost everything normal to them and thrown into our lives full of unknowns and new things that didn't feel right.

CONFUSION AND TEARS

It was a heartbreaking car ride as we continued to hear cries from the back seats. About halfway home the big kids started talking more and telling us about their visit. Jazmine started crying again as she remembered what had happened and the reality she was with us now. Jonathan looked over and said, "It's okay. Remember what Dad said." This made me curious, so I asked Jonathan what he was talking about. Jonathan, hesitant, told us Aaron had said they just needed to sign a paper and they were going to be moved to their grandma's house. Jonathan told me Aaron had said over and over, "I'll see you at grandma's tomorrow." As gently as possible we told the kids we didn't think it would be that easy. They didn't believe us. They thought they would be going to their grandma's house the next day.

This news was a startling discovery for Michael and me. *Could it be true? We had no idea the visit was coming, could a removal from our house happen so quickly as well?* It was another jolting experience in a full and emotionally-dense day. We got home and the kids settled into bed. The big kids both asked if me if I thought they were going to live with their grandma the next day. As kind and patient as possible, I explained to them "Your dad may have thought it was that easy, but I didn't think it would happen so quickly." The big kids went to bed with hopeful hearts expecting it was their last night with us. Christina still cried and screamed as I soothed her to sleep.

As soon as the house was quiet I started making phone calls to our state and agency workers. We hadn't heard anything about a grandma wanting the kids. I needed to let them know what the kids had told us about the visit. It was late so I had to leave messages. I heard from our state worker in the morning with great apologies. The judge had discovered a visit had happened and was very upset about this because the biological parents' court orders hadn't been fulfilled, mainly a clean drug test. Therefore, the visit shouldn't have happened and the worker said there would be no other contact until Madison and Aaron could produce a clean drug test. Not only that, but the kids wouldn't be going to live with their grandma. At least not so suddenly.

The kids were on edge all day continually asking if anyone had called to have them leave. We continued to tell them it wouldn't happen like they had hoped, and we told them we had even heard from the worker it wouldn't be happening. They continued to have hope though, until bedtime.

Bedtime was a clear realization we had been honest with them and they weren't going to be leaving. This bedtime was even worse than the first night for Jazmine. She knew they weren't leaving and it was not a pretty scene. She began kicking the wall and screaming, "I don't want to be here. I want to go back with my mom and dad. I want to live with my grandma. I don't want to be here." On top of soothing Jazmine, we still had Christina who screamed anytime we tried to get her to sleep. It took over an hour to get the girls both settled down and asleep.

Jonathan reacted differently than I expected. Instead of being sad, he began to feel angry. He said, "I don't know why I believed them. They are just liars. I can't believe anything they said. They don't really love us. Otherwise, we would be with them." I told him they did love them, but they had a lot going on and needed to take care of themselves so they could learn how to take care of them better. He didn't believe me, I could tell by the look he had on his face. He cried angry, hot tears onto his pillow as I patted his back and tried to sooth him.

There is one glimmer of hope from this instance. This was the beginning of many opportunities to build trust with the big kids. We had been honest with them and now they knew we had been honest with them, despite how hard the realization was for them. This was a big turning point, especially for Jonathan, in terms of bonding. It did, however, create more questions in his mind about why he was with us and why he had been told false statements about the length he would be with us.

Jonathan was eight years old, so he experienced this from a much deeper understanding than the other three did. He saw and remembered bad situations they had experienced with Madison and Aaron. He could see the difference in our house. He was starting to get a clear picture of what was safe and healthy and loving and how those characteristics compared with where he had come from. I think this was why Jonathan was always so grateful for our care and the life he had with us: he could feel the difference.

THE BEGINNING TURMOIL

The days following the visit brought on a side of the kid's we had yet to see, as their behaviors grew difficult. Jazmine was a mess. She had no idea what was going on, and it showed in her actions. She wouldn't accept answers she didn't like without a fight. She refused redirection. Her tantrums were increasingly disruptive and physical. I couldn't imagine how this little girl's heart was breaking.

We were beginning to see more anger within Jonathan. He started to talk back more and resist any correction. It seemed like he had realized his words were a tool he could use to make others hurt the way he did inside. He became more disrespectful to Jazmine, they could hardly be in a room together without arguments and fighting.

Michael and I began to see more clearly what amateurs we were at parenting. We quickly learned what worked and especially what didn't work. We made mistakes constantly as we navigated this road with Jazmine and Jonathan. It was on-the-job-training. Because we had no idea what we were doing, we gladly accepted advice from our workers. Tim recommended I read *1-2-3 Magic* after observing a parenting struggle during one of our weekly home visits. I quickly found myself a copy and read it within days. I prayed the method would provide more structure and consistency for the children, and make things easier for me too.

THE FIRST HOPE OF FOREVER

It was the night before the two-week anniversary of the kids coming into our home. It had not been a good day. Jazmine was still adjusting to being told what to do; boundaries, rules, and consequences for disobeying were not things she was used to. She had been in and out of time out all day long. It had been the worst day yet for discipline struggles. I was worn out and looking forward to bedtime. I had wondered several times throughout the day if I would make it through until bedtime.

I climbed up to Jazmine's bed on the top bunk and began reading her a couple of stories as she snuggled on my shoulder. We had been praying with the kids before bed and after I said a prayer, Jazmine looked at me and asked if she could pray too. I replied, "Yes! You can pray anytime, anywhere, because God always hears our prayers."

I watched her close her eyes and fold her hands. She bowed her head and prayed. She asked God if she could stay with us forever. Tears formed in my eyes as she said, "Amen." I hugged her tight while gaining my composure. When we were done hugging I looked in her eyes and said, "You can live with us as long as you need a safe place to stay, even if that means forever." I kissed her head, climbed down to the floor, and began patting her back as she fell asleep. I was in partial unbelief as I stood there in the dark. I wrapped my head around the idea that despite all the difficulties we had during the day, she seemed to be starting to form a bond with me.

I left her room shutting the door quietly behind me and the reality of her prayer made my heart overflow with joy. She didn't know what adoption was and she didn't know we wanted to adopt her. We had been very careful not to talk about adoption with or around the children. Yet, in her heart she knew she wanted to stay with us.

A MOMENT OF CONFIRMATION

We met our ongoing state worker, Terri, within a few weeks of the kids coming to live with us. I was filled with such anxiety as the meeting approached. I knew this person would have the power to lead and direct our case in great ways.

Terri came into our house and sat down. I made introductions and a cat jumped up next to her. I noticed she was acting somewhat uncomfortable as my cat tried to rub against her and say hello. "Does the cat bother you," I asked. "I'm actually allergic," she replied.

I felt terrible. I immediately moved our meeting to the backyard. I remember wrangling the kids into their shoes while holding Kyle, about a month old at the time. We made it to the backyard and I sat down feeling accomplished and ready to talk.

"I am just speechless," Terri said with a smile. "If I didn't know the situation, I would assume these were your children and that they had been with you since birth. Everything just feels so natural. I have never heard of children adjusting and easing into a foster home so well. Are you guys hoping this leads to adoption?"

At that moment, I felt every bit of what Terri said. It did feel completely natural to love and care for these four children, despite how hard it was and how utterly exhausted I had become.

Our first home visit went wonderful and we continued with monthly visits. Terri was an amazing resource and an excellent worker. She guided us and kept us as informed as possible about the children's case. I am so thankful for her and could not imagine having a better ongoing state worker.

AN UNINTENTIONAL LESSON LEARNED
Given their history with a lack of food, the kids were still often overeating at meals. I believe this was out of habit more than

anything. When they first came to live with us they were making far too many trips to the bathroom and often complained of tummy aches. Thankfully the tips from the initial doctor visit began to work.

Another food issue was their constant desire to have junk food. We had to teach them that certain foods were better for us to eat because they helped our bodies grow strong. Because of this we kept lots of fresh fruits and veggies in the house and several healthier crunchy options, like granola bars or nuts.

The kids continued to be amazed that people wanted to visit them and bring food. Each night they were excited to see whom they would meet and what they would bring for us to eat. One night, though, no one came. It was getting late so we decided to tell the kids they must have forgotten they were scheduled to bring food.

Before we could share what we were going to do about it, Jonathan asked, "So we aren't eating dinner tonight?" This was the perfect way to teach them there would always be food at our house. I shook my head, "Not at all. Even though someone forgot to bring us dinner, we still have food to eat." As I started to make dinner I could tell Jonathan's head was processing this information as he watched me prepare food for us. He realized, yet again, we were telling the truth.

Jonathan cried as he hugged me and said, "Thank you for

making dinner."

MY FIRST MOTHER'S DAY WITH CHILDREN

I had dreamed of my first Mother's Day for so long. I imagined it as an absolutely beautiful day full of joy and happiness. I wanted to celebrate the fact I had children to care for on Mother's Day, even if the kids weren't mine yet, they were at least with me for a time. I counted myself as their mother, even if only their *foster* mother. I loved them and I was growing more and more in love with them each day.

It was too soon to celebrate though. The wounds were too raw. I wanted the day to be about me finally being a mother, yet the kids were still hurting and grieving. This was the first big moment when I realized how selfish I really was. The kids were still in lots of pain, and didn't even consider me to be their mother. I had to lay aside my own ideas of what my first Mother's Day would look like and just be there for them.

The big kids knew it was Mother's Day. Although they couldn't verbalize how this holiday away from their mom made them feel, we saw their emotions, which overflowed through their actions throughout the day.

Jonathan felt the hurt of Mother's Day away from his biological mother the most. It was one of the first days when I took his words, aimed at me with an intention to hurt, personally.

"You aren't my mom and never will be," he yelled as he slammed his door in anger shortly before dinner. Something fell off of the bathroom shelf a second later and shattered as it hit the floor. I grabbed the broom and dustpan and knelt down to sweep up the pieces of glass. Through the wall, I could hear Jonathan sobbing in the next room. His heart, like the item I was cleaning up, was broken.

Jazmine's pain was more child-like. "I want my mom. I want my mom," she cried out in the midst of her tantrums. She kicked the wall hard over and over and screamed as loud as she could with a tear-drenched face.

After the kids were in bed, I collapsed into my own and cried hot tears into my pillow. The day's events had been complete agony. Being a mom was hard, harder than I had ever imagined. It hadn't been that long since the children had come to stay with us and we had already had an almost unbearable day. I wondered how I would survive another day like the one just ending. There was likely to be many more of them as our time together progressed.

About that time Michael came in and wrapped his arm around me. "Happy Mother's Day," he whispered. "I love you. It won't always feel like this."

Tears fell faster as he wrapped love around me with his arms. Despite my pain and despair, this simple act reminded me I had a reason to hope. God knew my pain. He gave me these children to care for and it was about Him and them, not me. God would use motherhood to continue to sharpen my heart and rid me of my deep-rooted selfishness. I will never be completely free of my selfish ways, but I would continue to see growth in this area as I learned more and more how to lay aside my own desires to care for the children the Lord had entrusted to me.

MARRIAGE IN THE MIDST OF THE CHAOS

As Michael and I adjusted to parenthood, we had to figure out how to maintain our marriage in the midst of the chaos. I spent almost every moment of my days with the children, giving them nearly everything I had in terms of energy. Michael would go to work and then come home at dinner ready to jump in and give his full attention to the kids. Once we finally got the last child to bed at night we were so worn out and tired we would often go to bed without having said as much as a word to one another.

Just as couples that have biological children wait several weeks before resuming intimacy, we found that weeks had passed and nothing had happened in the bedroom. I'm sure it was partially due to the stress, fear, and exhaustion of the situation, but we also weren't sure how to do this with children on the other side of shared walls so close by. We were overstimulated during the day and torn in so many different directions with the kids and managing the foster care side of things as well. Michael was likely struggling, as most men do, with his new role as husband and daddy and wondering where he fit in now that I had other people in our house to give my attention and time to.

We were navigating new waters in our marriage. We didn't realize how hard it would be to find time for each other in the midst of parenting. One day Michael hugged me and leaned in close.

"Are we ever going to have sex again?" he whispered in my ear.

I laughed and realized I had become so consumed with the care of the children that I had hardly thought about Michael's needs in our marriage. We were both giving so much during the day, yet we needed to figure out how to find the time and energy to give to our marriage and each other as well.

IN SICKNESS AND WITH LICE

Christina continued to struggle at every nap and at bedtime. Her behavior was also pretty erratic during the day as well. Given the fact she wasn't sleeping well and didn't understand what was going on, it was expected. Plus she was a toddler.

Thankfully I began to get used to her screaming fits. But I

noticed she was becoming more irritable and had started coughing and screaming even more. It became so bad that I began to get concerned that something was wrong under the surface, so I took her to the doctor.

The big kids were at school, so Kyle, Christina, and I headed to the doctor's office. Kyle hadn't taken a morning nap yet and was extremely fussy. He hadn't stopped crying since we had arrived in the waiting area. I unbuckled him quickly from his car seat and held him close. I bounced slightly on my feet making *shhh* sounds in an attempt to calm him down enough so that he could fall asleep. Christina was triggered by Kyle's crying and joined in with her loud screaming. She reached her arms up and grabbed at me begging me to pick her up too. I was quickly becoming an expert at holding two babies at the same time. Our name was called and the chaos was ushered into an exam room. The nurse helped me get there by holding our bags and Kyle's car seat as I carried both babies in my arms. Try as I might, I could not get them to settle down.

By the time the doctor entered the exam room I was feeling desperate and weary and it wasn't even ten o'clock in the morning. The doctor didn't seem to understand how hard life had been with a normally-difficult toddler who was even more difficult because she wasn't sleeping well and didn't feel good. Thankfully she didn't waste time and quickly ordered a variety of swabs to test for various illnesses. I left the doctor's office with two still-screaming babies. As soon as they were buckled in the car, I let the tears of utter desperation roll down my face as we drove home.

A few days later we heard back from the doctor and learned that Christina had Whooping Cough. We were all quarantined to our house and put on medicine for five days. We lived in a cozy 960-square-foot house. The six of us couldn't have contact with anyone else for those five days. *Have you ever heard of cabin fever?*

The Whooping Cough experience had a hidden blessing for Christina and me. You already know she had been a difficult child. I believe it had to do with her strong-willed nature and independence, and simply not being used to being taken care of. She had already, in her short life, learned to survive without much help. I later learned she had to learn to climb at a young age to find food. She also had to take her own diaper off when it was dirty in order for anyone to notice and change her.

It had been hard to bond with Christina because it seemed like I was constantly trying to calm her down during her screaming fits. I often had to hold her during her fits because she would throw herself on the ground and slam her head on the floor over and over. She would be kicking and screaming the whole time as I attempted to soothe her.

During the time she was sick, I was giving her baths more often and trying to sing and read to her more. I would hold her while she was wrapped in her towel, and she liked it. I would rub relaxing lotion on her to help calm her down, and she would actually smile at me. It was in these moments of caring for her when she didn't feel well that we started to bond, despite the frequent screaming fits throughout the rest of the day. I will always be thankful for this hidden blessing in the midst of the chaos of having a sick child.

Our family finished our medication for Whooping Cough when summer was about to begin and school was almost out. I didn't know how I felt about school being out. I hoped that less time driving back and forth between school and home would make our lives easier. Yet I was extremely worried about how Jazmine and Jonathan would do spending more time together. *Would I be able to keep the peace? Would I be able to keep going with all the kids, all day long, every day?*

I was still very much exhausted from everything life had thrown at us since the kids came into our lives. Each day I wondered if I would make it until bedtime so I could rest my weary body. I became more and more exhausted as each new day came, yet at the same time I constantly was able to find the strength to keep going. I tried to be excited for summer, despite my concerns.

Michael was going to be off of work for seven days and we had made it to the last day of school. I needed to get through the day before jumping headfirst into summer and all that it would bring our way. Then Jazmine started scratching her head.

I didn't think anything about it at first. But by lunchtime I had noticed her scratching so much that I was suddenly worried something was wrong. I had her sit in the kitchen at a place with good lighting and started inspecting her head. It didn't take long before I saw it. Lice. And lots of it.

Instinctively, I felt like scratching my scalp and I wondered if I had anything crawling around on my own head too. I started pacing the kitchen floor wondering what to do.

"We have lice. WE have lice. We have LICE!" The phrase was on repeat in my head, over and over it played.

I called Michael at work and we devised a plan. We needed to check everyone's head and get some of the special shampoo that kills lice. We needed to bag up our pillows, sheets, clothes, everything. We also needed to thoroughly clean the mattresses and carpet areas to make sure we didn't miss a single bug. In those first moments thinking about everything we needed to do, I felt frozen by the weight of the task. On top of everything we had already been through, now we had lice. It seemed like too much. I knew we couldn't do it alone. We were going to need help!

Through tears, I sent out a few desperate and embarrassed texts to friends asking if they would be able to come help us.

My friend Lauryn replied saying she would come right away and help however needed. She also offered to stop at the store and pick up the shampoo. Within the hour Michael was home from work and had picked Jonathan up from his last day of school. Soon after, Lauryn arrived with her husband Paul, both ready to help.

As the day went on and we did the dirty, nasty work of ridding our heads and home of lice, I was floored at the love my friends were showing us. *Can you imagine?* They came knowing they were going to be picking bugs off of our heads, bagging up our clothes and sheets which potentially had lice on them, and making sure we had no lice anywhere else in our house. I am still amazed they said yes.

While the adults were on lice duty, Jonathan and Christina played in the backyard since they were both free of lice. Michael set up the TV from our garage for when they needed some downtime. Kyle napped throughout the day in a bouncy seat.

Michael and Paul worked hard going from room to room bagging up all our clothes. While Michael was tending to Kyle a little while later, Paul sprinkled some disinfectant powder on our carpet and then vacuumed our entire house in great detail. All the while Lauryn was picking lice off of my head as I sat on the toilet in our small bathroom. Much like a "braid train" I participated in during middle school, yet much worse and not enjoyable at all. Lauryn worked on my head while I picked lice off of Jazmine's head.

I was already overwhelmed at the increase of laundry, dishes, and general household duties. Now we had an extra dose of chaos. I would literally need to wash every item of clothing in our house because we were taking every extra precaution to ensure all the lice was gone. I felt like I was going to drown in the pile of garbage bags that contained our clothes. The chaos was starting to close in on me.

I was thankful for Michael being home from work for the next several days. We were able to work together to find more peace in our home, and clean socks and underwear. Many times we have relied on each other to offer hope when life gets bleak. I can't imagine living this life with anyone other than Michael. Together, we always found a solution to our needs.

The Blessings Overflow
Chapter Four

There were many things that made life more chaotic with four children. The laundry. *Oh the laundry!* Have I mentioned we didn't have a dishwasher in our house? That's right. I was washing all the dishes by hand. It was actually becoming a relaxing ritual I performed after all the kids were in bed, when I had the energy at least. Then there's the cooking, the cleaning, the diapers, the toys. Life was much busier and full of chaos. As Lisa-Jo Baker wrote, "The glory of motherhood comes camouflaged in so much chaos."[2]

The overflow of laundry isn't just a sign of chaos, it is also a sign of more people in the house. The extra dishes show me I am feeding more mouths. The overflowing toys are a picture of the fun that fills our home. There are so many blessings to be found in the chaos of life.

___

[2] Baker, Lisa Jo. *Surprised by Motherhood: Everything I Never Expected about Being a Mom*. Carol Stream: Tyndale House Publishers, Inc, 2014. Kindle book.

I wrote this blog post nearly two months after the kids came to us:

> God is so good. Most days as I am caring for these children, just through regular interactions (like putting a nearly 15-month-old to sleep for her nap or feeding the two-month-old his bottle), I am overwhelmed at how He has filled our formerly quiet home and my formerly aching heart. Tears of joy and gratitude flow down my face regularly, even still after almost two months. My heart had been desiring to be a mother for so long, and it has been a long road to this point, but we are here.
>
> We have four children in our home we have been entrusted with the privilege and duty of caring for and nurturing. I had prayed so often when my heart was hurting for my trust to grow, trust that even though I thought I knew what was best, to lay aside my dreams and desires and trust in the goodness of the Lord and trust in the perfection of His plan.
>
> Now I am living His plan and I am in awe of how He has brought these children into our home. I often prayed the Lord would help me to see He can do far more abundantly than all I ask or think, and that He would help me realize my dreams are nothing compared to what He has planned for my life. How the Lord

answered my prayer and how wonderful His plans truly are!

My new life is blessed chaos. We are all starting to get comfortable and in our routines. It is becoming less chaotic (well, most days!) but still having a large family is a little chaotic just because there are six people in the house who need fed and clothed and cared for and transported here and there. Right?

The Lord is continuing to teach me about being present. At the beginning of this year I would have never imagined how the Lord would use this theme He placed on my heart to help me to live today and be present for every moment. You see, these children are here with us for now. We don't know how long they will be here. We are praying and hoping eventually this placement turns into an adoptive placement. Yet at this point it is completely temporary. We have no idea how long these precious children will be in our care.

I have learned a simple yet profound lesson. Today, in this moment, I am to care for these children. I am to love them today with no reserve. I am to focus on today and trust God for tomorrow and the next. I know this lesson will be valuable later in life. Aren't all children gifts from God that ultimately belong to Him? We are never guaranteed tomorrow. I am learning this truth and trying to live out my goal to be present this year, because I have to focus on today to get through.

BEAUTIFUL SUMMER DAYS AS A FAMILY

Our first summer with the kids held many wonderful memories. We heard Kyle giggle for the first time as he smiled wide-eyed at us. We experienced most of his "firsts" with tears and in awe of the opportunity to see growth and development in this way. Christina took her first steps in the beauty of the summer sun; wobbly, stunning, and brave.

In the busyness of life, sometimes the clock would suddenly display five and I had no plans for dinner. On these days, I would text Michael a plea to pick something up and he would often times come through the door with a family to-go meal from Salsarita's Fresh Cantina, a Mexican restaurant conveniently located on his way home. These fun, make-your-own taco nights were a favorite in our house that first summer filled with much chaos and many "Please pick up dinner" texts.

We would often find ourselves telling stories about our day, making jokes, and laughing so hard food would fall out of our mouths. Salsarita's tortilla chips have a seasoning on them which the children began affectionately referring to as "giggle dust." They hadn't experienced such meaningful mealtimes, so to them the tortilla chips were magic. Whenever we ate those delicious, easy-to-manage dinners, we would have wonderful family bonding over laughter and giggles.

Family meal times have always been a priority for us. Michael and I don't remember family meal times being a priority when we were growing up. We wanted to make sure it was a daily ritual with a deeper purpose for our children. Families bond and connect daily over the table with food. Our "giggle dust" dinners reminded me all the more of the children's craving for family, attention, and a more-normal life than they had lived previously.

A SUMMER OBJECTIVE

I do recall having one main goal for the big kids over that first summer: allow room for them to learn to be children. In a life where you don't have safe boundaries and no intentional supervision, you don't actually live. You only survive. The children had learned well how to survive, now it was time for them to learn how to live and be children.

I vividly remember the first time we played in the backyard. The big kids started fighting that one of them was Freddy Krueger trying to kill the other child in their dreams. They dashed across the yard so fast, I couldn't believe their speed. Once I caught on to the game and said I didn't like it too much, they started playing a different one where one of them was a zombie and their job was to try to kill the other one. Yikes! I needed a plan so they weren't just "killing" each other.

I created a loose summer routine that allowed a rhythm to our days and got us out of the house most mornings. I had lots of unstructured play time for the afternoons. I hoped it, along with the exposure to quality toys and books I had on hand, would help the kids learn to play. You see, I had noticed they didn't know how to do much of anything except watch television or play videos games. I believe it was a great act of God that we had decided to ditch our television to the garage before the kids came.

The kids would get bored with whatever they were doing quickly. I believe that low attention span is an effect of this technology-saturated culture we live in and their previous freedom to do and watch whatever they wanted for as long as they liked. I introduced them to new toys and activities one at a time and allowed them to move on to another activity when they were ready. I also started reading aloud to all four of them. Usually the babies would just be playing on the floor, but the big kids stayed interested for a little bit. We visited the library often and let the kids pick out their own books.

I also kept a stock of art supplies in the kitchen so the kids could be creative at the table between meals. Jazmine, one of the most creative children I've ever met, was often found at the table surrounded by a mess.

It was beautiful to see the children act out scenes from books we were reading and finally start playing pretend in a way that wasn't killing someone. I remember reading *A Bad Case of Stripes* and *The Three Grumpies* often. Jazmine would ask to eat lima beans and would draw pictures of people all different colors. Jonathan was reading many books, so much so I struggled to keep our library shelf stocked full enough for him. He was discovering a whole new world as he immersed himself in book after book.

A NEW NAME

It was during the summer chaos that an amazing blessing occurred. The big kids called me "Mom" for the first time. Since moving in, they had been asking us what we wanted them to call us. We had told them it didn't matter to us, they could call us whatever they would like. We had introduced ourselves as Ms. Ashley and Mr. Michael when we first met. They had been calling us those names for a few months.

Not long after Jazmine prayed she would stay with us forever, she would frequently pretend I was her mom and she was a baby. She craved normalcy. It was in the beginning of July she started calling me "Mom" (in real life, not just pretend play). She started calling Michael "Dad" shortly after that. We never wanted to pressure Jonathan to call us "Mom" and "Dad." We wanted to let him make the choice on his own and in his own timing.

Jazmine would give us hugs throughout the day and tell us she hoped she could stay with us forever. One time Jonathan asked, "Can we? Can we stay here forever?" This question prompted our first adoption conversation. I came down to their level and shared, "Your mom and dad are trying to get better. But, if your parents can't do what they need to do for you to go back to them, then you can stay here forever."

"Would we all be one family then?" Jonathan asked, "Like all have the last name Wells?"

Jonathan had a different last name from the other three children because he has a different biological father. This question was important because throughout his life he felt like he didn't belong since he had a different last name. He had continued to lack a sense of belonging at our house.

I remember during a training, before we had the kids, the instructor compared children in foster care to boats. Boats need an anchor to stay steady. They need a place to rest at the end of the journey. A safe haven from the waves and wind. Oftentimes children in foster care come to a new home without an anchor holding them down and steady in this world. They often feel lost and like they are just crashing through the waves of this big, scary world.

In that moment, I could see Jonathan was wanting confirmation we would be his anchor. He wanted to know he had a safe place to stay, away from the crazy world outside, no matter what. A place to keep him steady when waves come crashing in. I looked directly in his eyes with my hands cupping his face and replied, "Yes, we would be one big, happy family with the same last name."

It was shortly after this conversation I remember Jonathan gave me a hug and said, "I love you, Mom." Hearing him call me "Mom" for the first time was special because I knew he thought about it more and only did it when he was ready and comfortable. He never called me Ms. Ashley again.

THERAPY AND EXTRA SUPPORT

During that summer the children began therapy to help during the adjustment period. We wanted Jonathan to have extra help processing through his anger, and we needed help controlling Jazmine's frequent and intense tantrums. We did family therapy once a week throughout the summer. Our therapist, Bethany, helped Michael and I learn parenting skills and discipline methods that would help us manage the behavior problems that came our way. Bethany also met with the children for a short time individually and helped reinforce skills we were teaching them. They worked on not hitting, being kind and learned about accepting discipline without throwing a fit or getting angry.

Bethany continued to do therapy with the whole family through the fall, and then she began meeting with the kids one-on-one for longer sessions to help them work through their feelings about foster care and the adoption process. Jazmine also started seeing a second therapist, Whitney, during the winter to help her process some mild attachment struggles as well as behavior problems at school.

Before becoming a foster parent I had a fantasy-like idea of what therapy was like. Bethany and Whitney were instrumental, though, in helping the children adjust and process everything going on. They weren't laying on a couch sharing all their problems. The big kids didn't know how to verbally share how they felt inside. Instead, they would be on the floor playing games and Bethany or Whitney would ask intentional questions that would prompt answers to give a glimpse at what was going on in the children's hearts. They were both a great resource to Michael and me as we continued to learn about being parents.

Family Ties
Chapter Five

"We would like a placement that doesn't have any connections to their biological family. We aren't really wanting to have that kind of relationship." We said this in one of our initial meetings with the worker who approved our license to be foster parents. The thought of having to "share" our future children with relatives from their biological family and having something that tied us to our children's past terrified us.

Our worker looked at us with a concerned expression and responded, "What if there is an aunt or uncle who loves them and is safe for them, but can't take them into their family? We have lots of kiddos in situations like that. Would you consider a relationship then?"

We half-heartedly responded, "Of course. If it is in the children's best interest." I can tell you, though, sitting in that office we didn't actually mean it. We didn't want to have a continual tie to their former life. We voiced the right answer, yet we could never imagine having that kind of relationship.

Imagine our surprise when our state worker, Terri, brought up a grandma at one of our monthly home visits. She wanted to know if we were willing to arrange a meeting so the children's grandma could get to know us and see the children. This was the same grandma Aaron had been talking about from the visit the first week we had the kids. We were nervous, but Terri assured Michael and me she knew confidently this grandma had a soft heart for these kids and wanted very much to meet the people who were caring for them. With great hesitancy and concern, we trusted Terri and said we would meet Grandma Susie.

A few weeks later, on a Saturday, we drove to a nearby McDonald's restaurant. The kids had been anxiously awaiting the day they would get to see their grandma again. This grandma had been worried about the kids, calling Terri often, and wanted to see with her own eyes who was taking care of them and if they were in a home where they were loved and felt safe. It was one of the longest car rides of my life, yet in reality only lasted ten minutes. I was sitting in the passenger seat of our van, my stomach in knots, thinking about what this woman was going to be like.

I knew this was an important person in our children's lives, although I didn't know the extent of the impact she would have in my own life as well. So many thoughts were running through my mind. *What if she didn't like us? What would she think about the kids calling us mom and dad? Would she support us in front of the kids? Would she see how much we love her grandchildren? Would she tell their biological mother and father about us? What would she say to them?*

I took great caution as we unloaded the car and I gripped the children's hands tightly as we walked toward the entrance. As we neared the door I saw her waiting and watching. As Grandma Susie laid eyes on the children I could see her eyes start to water and she couldn't hold back the large smile that soon appeared on her face. Obviously her heart was so happy to see them. The big kids shouted "Grandma!" as we opened the door and they ran into her arms. The smiles were so wide and beautiful.

Grandma Susie took a break from hugging the kids and walked over to embrace me. As she held me she whispered through tears, "*Thank you.*" We ordered lunch and made our way to the play place. The kids stayed close to Grandma Susie wanting to enjoy each moment they had with her. We ate lunch as the kids shared stories of their new life with us. Jonathan was talking about his summer golf lessons and Jazmine shared how excited she was to start school.

As everyone finished eating Grandma Susie asked the kids to go play so she could talk to us. I thought, *"Oh no, here's the moment of truth."* She held Christina in her arms, eyes in awe of how big she had gotten, then she stared at us and asked boldly, "So, if you got the chance would you adopt them? All of them?" Michael and I looked at each other. We didn't know what to say. We hadn't expected this question, at least not right away. Terri was coming to meet us and was running late. We told Grandma Susie we didn't know if we could talk about adoption and we wanted to wait until Terri got there to clarify if we could respond. Grandma Susie apologized for being so direct, and then went on to say she believed the kids deserved better and she had lost hope that Madison and Aaron could get better. "My priority now is for the kids to be happy and loved," she told us.

Once Terri arrived, we told her what Grandma Susie asked us and wondered if it was okay to answer. Terri said we were allowed to talk about anything we were comfortable with, it was up to us. Michael looked at me as if telling me to go ahead and answer. I surveyed the play place as the children played happily and then turned back to look at Grandma Susie.

"We have prayed for the chance to be parents for years," I told her. "We would love the chance, if given, to adopt these children and love them for the rest of their lives just as if we had given birth to them. Our goal in fostering is to adopt and give children a permanent home."

I couldn't hold back the tears as I shared my heart.

Grandma Susie smiled wide, with a sense of relief in her eyes, and said, "Whew. That makes me so happy. It's obvious the kids are happy and feel loved. They look rested and calm for the first time in their lives, and they call you Mom and Dad so naturally." As I listened to her joy, I was so overwhelmed with emotion. She hugged me again and told me how happy she was to finally meet us and see everything Terri had told her about us to be true.

Grandma Susie and I shared a love for these children. As we loaded the car after the visit, she hugged me again with tears in her eyes. She whispered in my ear, "The kids are right where they belong and this is exactly where they need to stay."

A VISIT TO OHIO

With it being summer break, it was the perfect time to take a trip to Ohio and introduce the children to most of our family who hadn't been down to visit yet. Our first and, at the time, only niece was turning two and on the same day there was a surprise party for Michael's grandma and grandpa who were celebrating fifty years of marriage. It would be a busy day, but we very much wanted to show off these kids who had stolen our hearts. Plus, three hours isn't too far to travel.

We loaded the van bright and early at six o'clock and were glad when most of the kids went back to sleep for at least a little bit. A McDonald's stop came at the perfect time, just before eight. We fed Kyle, changed diapers, and let everyone stretch their legs on the play place. We got back in the van about thirty minutes later and were ready to push through the second half of the trip. We arrived just as planned to the surprise brunch before ten o'clock! It was exciting for the children to not only meet everyone but to also ask questions about why we were celebrating. We loved sharing with the children about why marriage is worth celebrating.

To see Michael's grandma embrace the children with such happiness was beautiful. As I walked toward her holding Kyle with the other children following close behind, her face lit up as she reached out and hugged each one of them. They were her great-grandchildren in those first moments, even though nothing was official. She spoiled them with hugs and kisses, just as grandmas do. It warmed my heart to witness such open hearts for the children.

The birthday party afterward was just as much of a success. Many of my relatives were there and we even got to see some unexpected guests who made it even better. The little ones both napped for a portion of the event and the big kids enjoyed playing in the swimming pool on the hot and sticky July afternoon.

As we made our way to the last stop of the day, a quick visit with Michael's mom and other family, the big kids were wearing down, as were the adults. Jazmine and Jonathan loved meeting their Uncle Evan (Michael's brother), who was only six years old. Yes, six years old. Michael's mom and stepdad had another child soon after we married. Uncle Evan fit in perfectly right between Jonathan and Jazmine, which they all thought was the funniest thing ever!

We loaded the van dressed in pajamas and ready for all the kids to drift sweetly to dreamland. We were all tired but also so happy with full hearts. The first twenty minutes went as planned, *then chaos entered our minivan.*

Christina (our resident screamer) started screaming as she fought sleep. Her screaming was keeping Kyle up. The big kids were starting to complain, you know the common pleas, "I'm hungry! I'm tired! My ears hurt! Make it stop!!!" By this point, this momma, who was in the back as the peacekeeper, was starting to feel overwhelmed. I could feel the tension rising within me. I was purposefully taking deep breath after deep breath and struggling to keep my cool while I attempted to soothe Christina.

We made our first stop an hour into the trip after forty minutes of non-stop screaming. We rearranged people in an attempt to help the children get the sleep they so desperately needed and the quiet I craved more than anything at that moment. Twenty minutes later, after more screaming, we attempted to rearrange the seats again. Twenty minutes later (again), we stopped to feed Kyle, who was way past the point of exhaustion, and we also tried rocking Christina to sleep. We got the big kids snacks then too. I prayed, "Please, Lord, help the kids go to sleep. We are so tired."

We loaded back in the van to see if full bellies and relaxed cuddling helped ease the kids into sleep. Thirty more minutes of constant screaming and whining and we had to stop again. We had been on the road for almost three hours and had not even traveled a third of the way through our three-hour journey home. We were at a gas station, all six of us completely exhausted. I was about to pull my hair out.

I climbed over the children (literally) from the back of the van to be the first person to get out and walked very quickly, okay, *more like ran as if my life depended on it,* into the gas station bathroom where I cried for fifteen minutes behind the locked door. I was so overwhelmed and tired. I didn't know how I was going to continue this trip.

I walked back to the van with puffy eyes, head looking toward the ground, awaiting the sound of screams. As I got closer I was amazed. It was quiet. I opened the door and saw that Kyle was drifting to sleep, and Christina was working on it as well. Jonathan and Jazmine weren't even looking at me, so I knew they had been warned it was now time to stop whining and complaining and go to sleep for everyone's sake.

Within fifteen minutes, all the kids were finally asleep and I shut my eyes to sleep as well. This was definitely not how we planned our journey home. Yet it was a great lesson that things don't always go the way you expect or plan. Sometimes, you just need a good cry and then you realize it will all be okay.

LET'S TRY THIS AGAIN

We didn't let the first trip to Ohio haunt us forever. Three months after that chaotic car ride we decided to try again.

We went to Ohio with two main goals this time. First, we were going to visit our former church to celebrate its fiftieth anniversary weekend. This is the church where Michael and I were both baptized and married. Many of my family attends there so we got to visit with them as well as with old friends. After the church celebration, we spent quality time with Michael's family because we hadn't seen them very long the last time.

We hadn't been to our former church since the kids came, so nearly everyone was meeting our kids for the first time. These are many of the people who journeyed through the years of infertility with us and saw the years waiting for children through adoption without avail. They knew us and our story. It was incredibly encouraging to see the people who had prayed for us warmly embrace our children and tell us how happy they were for our family.

These were *our* people. They knew our former hurt; but now they saw the pure joy and blessings that overflowed from our lives. Many people came to us at the gathering to meet our kids and share about how they were so encouraged by our journey. People came to give us hugs and shed a few tears because they were seeing the Lord bless our family by adding these four children. It was an act of coming full-circle to be at our old church with children.

Spending time with Michael's family was equally encouraging. Our kids loved hanging out with their Uncle Evan again. Michael's mom and stepdad fit the role of grandparents so wonderfully, even more than last time. We played games, laughed a lot, and talked about how parenthood was treating us.

On our way home, we got in the van and I took a short nap. *Yes!* All the kids were quiet and let me nap for fifty miles. After I woke, we shared dinner together while I fed Kyle some squash and his bedtime bottle. We reached our halfway point right around bedtime and Kyle was already asleep. We had been more prepared with our laptop this time and put *Winnie the Pooh* on. Within thirty minutes Christina was asleep too!

Jazmine was scared because it was dark and the trees on the side of the road looked very conspicuous. She held my hand the entire movie. It was sweet and precious. This girl, she melts my heart. *Oh, who am I kidding?!? They all melt my heart!* After the movie, we passed out pillows and the big kids also went to sleep quickly, with Jazmine leaning on my shoulder and gripping my hand.

After a short time, I was staring up into the sky gazing at the stars. I wish in those moments I had been in the front of the van next to Michael instead of in the back. I wanted to reflect together upon our time in Ohio and life in general. Instead I had to reflect alone. I was overcome with joy at how I was so abundantly blessed.

The song "10,000 Reasons (Bless the Lord)"[3] came on the radio and I started weeping. You must know by now this whole journey made me an emotional ticking time bomb. I never knew when or what would set me off.

> *Bless the Lord, O my soul*
> *O my soul*
> *Worship His holy name*
> *Sing like never before*
> *O my soul*
> *I'll worship Your holy name*

I couldn't contain my emotions. Not after the amazing trip filled with meaningful encouragement, such a smooth ride home, and all my sleeping children within three feet of me. My heart was full of pure gratitude toward God Almighty who made all of this possible! How could I not sit there and weep

---

[3] Redman, Matt. "10,000 Reasons (Bless the Lord)." *10,000 Reasons.* sixstepsrecords/Sparrow Records, 2011.

while I sang the words my heart felt so clearly?

> *You're rich in love, and You're slow to anger*
> *Your name is great, and Your heart is kind*
> *For all Your goodness I will keep on singing*
> *Ten thousand reasons for my heart to find*

Ten thousand reasons. I will sing.

The Roller Coaster Begins
Chapter Six

I had no idea what to wear. What do you wear when you are going to court and will be meeting for the first time the biological mother of the children you love and would be honored to adopt? I was in Lane Bryant trying on outfit after outfit looking for one that was nice, but not too nice, but made me look put together and not so exhausted, but not over the top. What a difficult feat! The ladies working that particular night were kind as I kept asking their opinions and hoping they would help me find just the right clothes to wear.

I was nervous from my toes to the tips of my hair. It was the first court date I was going to be able to attend. (There had been one shortly after the kids were placed with us, but I didn't learn it about it early enough to arrange child care.) We couldn't find a sitter for the upcoming court date so Michael requested off work and stayed at home with the children while I attended court alone.

I wouldn't necessarily be alone, because all the workers were going to be there, however I wanted someone there for me. So I asked my friend Lauryn (the one who helped us when we had lice) to come with me. Lauryn wasn't really there for any reason except to help me get through the waiting. She was there for pure emotional support.

There was a long list of cases on the morning's docket. The court officer would call the cases one by one and only when we were called would we go into the courtroom. The waiting area was large and open and reminded me of an airport terminal with rows of chairs and people constantly coming, going, and simply waiting. We had no idea when it would be our turn.

Lauryn and I sat down near the courtroom entrance and watched as people walked by. Their facial expressions varied as much as their characteristics. Many seemed to be anticipating a difficult outcome, their faces looked heavy burdened. Shortly after we arrived, Tim and Angela (Angela was now our agency worker and Tim had come for extra support) came and sat down by us. Then Terri (our state worker) arrived and greeted us. Terri didn't stay long and then went into a separate waiting area for state workers and attorneys. She came out a little later and introduced me to the children's guardian ad litem named Carol. Carol was a volunteer court-appointed attorney whose sole purpose was to represent and fight in court for the children and their best interest.

Carol was friendly and encouraging as well. She told me there had been no tangible progress on the biological parents' court orders and she would be urging the court to commit the children into state's care. I didn't understand what this meant, except it would give the state the freedom to start moving toward terminating parental rights (TPR) because of the lack of progress.

After talking to Carol I sat back down next to Lauryn and waited. I could hardly breathe. Madison and Aaron weren't there yet, but Terri had talked to them that morning and they said they would be there. I kept looking toward the elevators thinking any minute they would walk out and be right there, right in front of me. *What would I say? What would they say? Would they sit by us? How much longer were we going to have to wait?*

You could look around the room and sense the tension on everyone's faces. I can only imagine the reasons that brought each person there that particular morning. There was one woman in particular who was not having a good day. She was gaining nearly everyone's attention throughout the morning with sobs and moaning. I was nearby her and overhead talk of terminating parental rights. The devastation of losing custody of her children permanently was obvious, especially to those nearby her.

It was heartbreaking to be so close to her in those moments, watching her world fall apart, and yet the reason I was in my seat was because I was caring for someone else's children and here on their behalf. That could have well been Madison one day, crying out in agony over how her life choices have been the cause of her children being taken away. I had to close my eyes and focus on my breathing for a few moments.

I remembered what Aaron looked like from meeting him at the visit we had right after getting the kids. When I saw him walk off of the elevator I lost my breath for a moment. Walking right behind him was whom I could only imagine to be Madison, the children's biological mother. As soon as I saw her I could see many of Jonathan's features in her face, it was surreal. Terri saw them arrive as well and walked over to them and talked for a few minutes.

As soon as they all turned toward me I could feel my hands get clammy and began to shake. Terri introduced us to each other and suddenly the arms that had held my children when they were minutes old wrapped around me in the busy waiting area.

"Thank you," Madison said as she embraced me with heavy tears in her eyes.

She was only about a foot away from me, and I was thankful when she backed up a little bit. She began asking me a few questions about the kids and I shared the milestones they had achieved since meeting them four months earlier.

With tears soaking her face she began telling me how happy she was to finally meet me and how sorry she was for how bad things had gotten. She also shared she was working on getting herself together.

"I've made a few mistakes, but I'm working on fixing them," she said.

I had no words. I just smiled gently at her, nodding my head. I wasn't expecting such friendliness, or blatant unawareness of the seriousness of the situation.

Addiction is a powerful force in a person's life. Madison and Aaron's addiction to drugs had interfered with their life so much that their kids had been taken away. Yet, just that reality wasn't enough to overpower the addiction. Despite having their children removed from their home, the addiction still ruled their lives, rendering them unable to do what was necessary to get their life back on track.

I was only seeing a shell of the woman Madison used to be. It was earth-shattering to see how addiction had taken over this woman's life and up until this point, how she'd been unable to fight against the urges that came even when getting her children back was on the line. Addiction was stealing her children, her smile, and the life she once knew.

As they walked back to their seats across the room, I let out a deep exhale and tried to sort through all the feelings crowding my mind. I could still feel my insides trembling from nerves. They sat about thirty feet from me while we waited. I would do my best to talk to Lauryn and keep my mind off of the fact they were there, yet I just couldn't shake the anxiety. Every time I glanced at them they were watching me. I did my best to smile and appear as if I was fine. I wondered what they were thinking about me and if they could tell, even though our conversation was brief, how much I loved the children.

Shortly after one o'clock the last case on the docket was finally called, ours.

THE COURTROOM EXPERIENCE

We were only in the courtroom for ten minutes, it went by so quickly. Terri and Carol sat at the table on the left with Tim, Angela, and me in the benches behind them. On the right side sat Madison and Aaron with their respective attorneys. Lauryn had to stay in the waiting room since she was not involved in the case.

We stood up as the judge entered the room and then sat down. The judge began by asking Carol for an update on the case. She spoke kindly of Michael and me and honestly about new revelations we had learned since the children were with us about their life before being removed from their biological parents' care. In closing, she suggested to the judge to commit the children into the state's care. The judge moved to Terri and asked if she had anything to add. Then the judge moved on to the biological parents' attorneys for confirmation of the status update. The judge spoke sternly and directly to Madison and Aaron, sharing her disappointment at the lack of progress. The judge granted the request for the children to be committed into state's care.

"Can you tell me about the kids? How are they doing?" The judge asked, looking at me. I spoke with both joy and trepidation as all eyes were turned to me and I shared about each child and the progress they were making in our home. It was awkward to speak about the children, the children I loved and hoped to adopt, while their biological parents sat ten feet from me.

The judge smiled at me and then surveying the room asked if anyone else had anything to add. Carol spoke confidently and said, "I'd like it to be noted the children are placed in a concurrent home." The judge nodded and then asked for all parties to leave the courtroom except for our agency workers, the state worker, and all attorneys. Basically, she wanted me and the biological parents to leave the courtroom so she could talk to everyone else about something involving the case, I assume.

I walked out of the courtroom and the biological parents walked out behind me. I sat down with Lauryn and wondered if

I should leave or wait for everyone else to come out of the courtroom. Aaron walked back toward where they had been sitting, but Madison sat directly opposite from me with her head in her hands.

As Lauryn and I were getting ready to leave, Madison walked over to us. She boldly asked me a question that you could tell she was scared to know the answer to.

"When the attorney mentioned that the kids are in a concurrent home does that mean you would adopt them?" she asked with distress in her voice.

My heart skipped a beat and the room seemed to be still all at once as she looked at me waiting for the answer. No one was around and I had no idea how to answer her question. My heart was racing and pounding in my chest. I had to hold my hands together because they were shaking so badly. I was worried if I didn't stop the shaking my whole body would lose control.

I took a deep breath and as sympathetically as I could and with a soft voice I responded.

"Yes. When Michael and I were licensed we said we would be open to adoption if the children placed in our home ended up needing a permanent home," I said. I didn't smile.

I did my best to continue breathing slowly and keep myself from convulsing from the anxiety of the situation. Madison looked at me with puffy eyes and her breathing became heavy. In that moment I knew she understood for the first time there was another option for her children other than returning to her.

By answering her question I altered her entire mindset and broke her spirit. She sat back down and started sobbing loudly as everyone else exited the courtroom. Terri and Tim rushed over and asked what happened. As soon as I told them, Tim looked at me and suggested it was time to make our exit. As we walked onto the elevator we could still hear her heavy sobs and at that moment I carried the burden of breaking her heart.

THE MONTHS THAT FOLLOWED

We were told after we left that Aaron mentioned voluntarily terminating his parental rights. We were also told Madison was thinking about it too. She had told Terri that watching me reminded her of who she used to be before she had taken such a drastic change of direction in her life. She had said it made her happy to see me smile and laugh and know the kids were with someone so full of life.

It felt like we were on pins and needles as we waited to hear what would happen next. *Would they see our deep love for the children and voluntarily TPR to allow us to adopt the kids? Or would they have a greater motivation to make the necessary changes and get the kids back?*

The most difficult thing about the waiting was not knowing what was going on. It was as if we were playing a game of telephone, where one person says something to someone else and then by the time it is passed through person after person the truth is distorted and unclear. We oftentimes had no idea what was going on with the biological parents because the news changed so often.

It was during this time we began the typical "roller coaster" experience, which is often used to describe this season of fostering. One week we would hear great news and then the next week we would hear news completely contradictory to the previous update. All we could do was try not to make ourselves sick thinking about it and just love the kids as best we could each day whether it was a high or low moment. At least we had them to distract us from the ebb and flow of updates. As hard as it was, we were thankful for each day we could love them.

The difficult reality of the roller coaster stage is this: as much as you go up and down, you are still living your life full of chaos with the children who are counting on you for stability. You don't get a break right away to process the updates. You hear news, and in the next room are children waiting for you. You have to act normal, like whatever you heard didn't affect you, and continue reading books or playing games. It's agonizing to hold in the roller coaster of emotions you are experiencing while also attempting to remain a constant, unchanging parent to the children.

Not only that, but when there is news of even the *idea* of progress with the biological parents, it shakes your reality. You're oftentimes living life, feeling like a "normal" family when you hear news that reminds you nothing in this process is guaranteed. I prayed often, "Lord, please give Madison and Aaron the wisdom to know what to do. Either help them fight, or help them let go gracefully in love. This roller coaster is just too much to handle. I want it to end and have confidence and know where I am going to be when it is all over."

I so relate to Jennie Allen when she writes, "To risk is to willingly place your life in the hand of an unseen God and an unknown future, then to watch him come through. He starts to get real when you live like that."[4] God was becoming more and more real as we found ourselves risking everything we knew in life and trusting Him with the future.

Near the end of October, two months after court, the state changed the children's permanency goal from reunification to adoption. This was a great step forward. When children are first put in the foster care system their permanency goal is

---

[4] Allen, Jennie. *Anything: The Prayer That Unlocked My God and My Soul.* Nashville: Thomas Nelson, 2012. Kindle book.

always reunification. In our case, after six months of the children being with us and no progress from the biological parents, the state changed the goal. This wasn't a legal change, it just meant in the state's eyes they saw the case moving more toward adoption than reunification.

After the state made this change Terri filed the necessary paperwork to get a TPR date. All we could do was wait for our paperwork to be processed and then we would be notified of a court date.

First Birthdays and the Holidays
Chapter Seven

As school was well underway and holidays were starting to approach, things started to heat up in the house. The summer had contained its full share of chaos, though most of it was adjustment related. By now, we were all feeling more comfortable with each other, but the kids had started to show more typical foster care related behaviors: lying, stealing, angry outbursts, continued intense tantrums, as well as occasional grief. I was so thankful family therapy was already happening regularly, which made beginning individual therapy with Bethany for each of the big kids a smoother transition.

Months stretched and there wasn't any tangible case-related information to share with the children. Jazmine and Jonathan didn't understand what was happening under the surface. The children were, more often than not, left in the dark as they wondered what was going to happen with their permanency. Michael and I were right there with them in the waiting and wondering. *What was our daily life going to become? Would the children return to Madison and Aaron? Or would we get the opportunity to adopt these children into our family?* These thoughts hardly left my mind.

During the summer months, Michael and I were adjusting to being new parents, not only to an infant but to a toddler, an almost-school-aged daughter, and a school-aged son. There was a lot of trial and error on our part. We were learning to set boundaries and share expectations, and then also give redirections or appropriate discipline when those boundaries were broken or expectations were not met. In the first few months we learned about the importance of structure, consistency, and routine. We were beginning to see real positive change.

Yet during those summer months the children were mostly in honeymoon mode still. Yes, we had tantrums, yes we had sibling arguments, and yes we thought it was crazy hard. *Oh, if we only knew what was in store for us.* Jonathan was unquestionably in the honeymoon stage more than Jazmine was. But Jazmine still seemed to be restrained slightly and testing the waters of our home. The little ones weren't old enough to understand what was going on. Christina was still proving to be more difficult than the average toddler. She continued to throw regular, multiple-times-a-day, Hulk-sized fits.

Near the middle of October we started seeing glimpses of more difficult days ahead of us. We knew things would continue to get worse before they got better. I mean, the honeymoon was bound to end and we would face some pretty big feelings from Jonathan and Jazmine. These feelings were buried down deep inside of their hearts and would come unearthed eventually.

We found ourselves wondering each day what was going to come to the surface, whether it was another realization of the neglect they had faced before, or a new behavior to learn to deal with. Life was quite unstable now with children working through the reality of foster care and possibly not returning to their biological parents. Michael and I never knew what the day would bring and what new obstacles we would face through the process.

It started with nightmares: vivid, feels-too-real-to-be-fake, wake-up-screaming-with-a-wet-bed, kind of nightmares. They mostly stemmed from too-scary movies the big kids had been exposed to previously.

Jazmine had a recurring nightmare that terrified her. She dreamed of a hand reaching toward her and snatching her off of her bed while she was sleeping. Then, in the nightmare, she would be taken to some sort of dungeon where she was tied to a table. We would hear her screaming from her bed. Jazmine would be shaking and have tears rolling down her face by the time I came to embrace her, often every night. As I held her tightly I'd said over and over, "It's okay. It wasn't real. You're here with me. You're safe." I'd brush my fingers through her hair and rub her back as she hid her face in my shoulder. I'd often rock her gently back to sleep trying to ease the fear that had captured her.

Jonathan's dreams tied more to scary movies like *The Texas Chainsaw Massacre* and *A Nightmare on Elm Street*. We assumed these dreams were triggered by Halloween. We made the decision to avoid all things Halloween with the kids, including stores with seasonal aisles and streets decorated over-the-top.

Michael and I began to feel downright exhausted again each day from these frequent nighttime events. We didn't think it was possible to feel more tired, but the fatigue continued to increase. The big kids had a heightened sense of awareness for their surroundings and again started to fight bedtime for fear of what they would face once they found themselves asleep.

Near the beginning of November, when the nightmares were mostly under control, we began to see struggles with blue-feeling days. Days when the kids, especially Jonathan, just couldn't shake off the sad feelings attempting to overtake him. These were days when they wondered what Madison and Aaron were doing and why they hadn't heard from them yet. These were difficult days when attempts at soothing, on Michael and I's part, made no difference.

Jonathan started to distance himself from us and walked around with a hint sadness no matter where he was. He was struggling deeply with the reality he might not see his parents again, which meant that they weren't fighting for him like they said they would. Michael and I would often tell Jonathan, as his heart was breaking right in front of us, they were doing the best they could. We would say, "Drugs make people so sick in their head they can't do what they need to do or take care of things even if they want to." School was a great distraction during these struggles.

LEANING ON EACH OTHER

By the middle of November, still 2012, both of the big kids were struggling. Michael and I were facing one thing after another and were exhausted beyond anything we had ever experienced in our lives. Most days as I put the little ones down for a nap I would fall into my bed and rest as well.

Michael would often come home from work, spend time with the kids, and then go to bed right after we tucked the last child in for the night. I applauded him for even being able to be "all there" with the kids after dinner despite being at work all day long. He didn't know how I kept going each night despite being with the children all day and whatever additional activities we had, like therapy, home visits, or doctor's appointments.

But God continued to give us just enough energy to get

through each day. We were thankful to have each other as well. When I had particularly rough days, Michael would come home from work and try to give me some relief. Then when Michael became overwhelmed with the task at hand, loving these children despite how they were feeling or acting, I would be right there to help.

We saw the beautiful truth from Ecclesiastes 4:9-10 come to life in our marriage in a way it never had.

> Two are better than one, because they have a good reward for their toil. For if they fall, one will lift up his fellow. But woe to him who is alone when he falls and has not another to lift him up!

We were so thankful to be in this together. Despite the struggles we faced, we could lean on one another in our time of need.

I believe there is a stigma that plagues parents with kids who have difficult behaviors. In our struggles with the kids, Michael and I found it difficult to be honest and reach out to those around us for help. *Would they still love our children if they knew how deeply they were struggling with their behavior? Would we still be accepted [in our church, at play group, in our family, etc...]? Would people think we weren't cut out for this parenting gig? Would we be condemned for our children's behaviors?*

Because of the fear of what others would think, we lost a piece of community that would have been extremely helpful in these exhausting times. If I had been so bold to ask for help or even to simply open up and talk about how I was feeling, maybe I wouldn't have felt so alone in the midst of struggles.

ANOTHER DIFFICULT SEASON

Jazmine was starting to act out at school and began seeing a second therapist each week that worked with her to control her behavior. Jazmine's tantrums were growing more intense from the fits we had seen over the summer. Whitney, the second therapist, was the first person to bring up the reality of a mild attachment disorder as well as Jazmine's difficulty with transitions.

Whitney helped Michael and I understand Jazmine had built a wall around all the sad feelings she had about being separated from her biological parents, as well as the hope that one day she would return to them. The longer she stayed with us, the more she felt love for us, and the wall was starting to crumble and cause all sorts of feelings and chaos inside of her she didn't know how to cope with. Because of this, the chaos overflowed into her behavior and out of control tantrums and outbursts.

Jonathan had just had his first birthday with us, he was nine now, but unfortunately it was a difficult awareness that he was still with Michael and I and apart from his biological parents.

"I knew it. I just knew I would still be here on my birthday," he said to me through tears. One day he would be asking if we could adopt him and then the next day be in tears when seeing a billboard for a brand of beer because it reminded him of his biological parents. Jonathan was experiencing the same sort of chaos inside as Jazmine was.

Bethany, our main therapist, told us that children around Jonathan's age may start to feel happy about their foster home and want to be adopted. But at the same time they feel like they are wrong because they should want to go back to their biological parents. Jonathan wanted to stay with us, but then he would feel as if he were violating natural, deep-rooted loyalties to his biological parents at the same time. He was happy, yet he was grieving.

There weren't many tangible actions we could do or words to say to help the children feel better. We just needed to continue to be there, loving and caring for them no matter what they threw our way. The kids needed to work through their feelings.

Bethany said some of the behavior was purely to test if we really were who we said we were. Jazmine and Jonathan needed to be sure we were committed to them, no matter what. Subconsciously, they may have been testing to see if there was any behavior that would make us stop loving them or send them away.

As an adult I felt so overwhelmed with the process, the waiting, and the unknown. Yet I watched these children struggling with even more intense feelings. I could hardly handle all my feelings. How were they, young children, supposed to handle all the thoughts and feelings that circulated through their minds and hearts on a daily basis?

Something the kids worked on, Jonathan especially, during therapy was learning to identify and express the specific feelings they had. Children raised in difficult places don't often have a vocabulary and understanding of different feelings. Most know happy and sad and angry, but they don't know many other feelings or how to help themselves feel better when they experience these emotions.

Jonathan was learning the differences between his feelings as well as new words to explain other emotions he felt. We made a list with him of different feelings, as well as activities that could help him when he felt a certain way. This was useful because he was soon able to use words to describe how he was feeling inside. Once he could communicate how he was feeling, he wasn't alone in his frustration or grief or fear or worry. We were able to help him acknowledge how he felt and begin moving past the feeling together.

A practical tool that helped many times during this season was using a sheet of paper with a large heart drawn on it. We would have the children color it in with specific colors which reflected how they were feeling. Jazmine couldn't verbally share how she was feeling, and Jonathan was still learning to open up about how he felt. Yet when we handed them a red crayon and asked to draw on their heart how angry they were, it was giving them the opportunity (and teaching them as well) to express their feelings[5].

At home we started teaching the kids the importance of prayer. We wanted them to know that God heard their prayers wherever they were and whatever they had to say. We described how God is our Heavenly Father and wants to take care us. We often explained to Jonathan what a burden was and how our worries can become a heavy burden to carry. Then we would tell him God wanted to carry our burdens and wanted us to cast our cares on Him because He cares for us, just as 1 Peter 5:7 says. This was when Jonathan became more interested in the Bible and learning about God and the Good News of Jesus Christ.

IT WAS ALL TOO MUCH

When Jonathan's honeymoon ended, it was like a volcano erupted and exploded everywhere. We got a phone call from the school and we suddenly became more aware of the deep pain, guilt, and confusion Jonathan was experiencing.

---

[5] We got this idea from Carol Lozier's "Colors of my Heart" tool, which can be found here: http://www.forever-families.com/colorsapp.html.

We got the call about two hours before dismissal for that particular day. The principal asked us to come and pick Jonathan up early. She said he had been crying uncontrollably in the office for hours. They had been trying to calm him down, and maybe he would take a few relaxing breaths for a moment, but then it would come back full force.

An incident happened in his classroom where he had hurt another child's feelings and seeing that child hurt and visibly upset triggered all the feelings he had been holding back and avoiding for the last seven months. Once it started, he just couldn't stop. We rushed to the school and called our main therapist, Bethany, as we got closer and asked if she could swing by the house to check in and help us figure out what to do next.

Jonathan was able to calm down slightly once we arrived at school and I wrapped my arms around him. He kept saying, "I'm sorry. I didn't mean to. I can't stop crying." On the car ride home he seemed more at peace until I asked, "Jonathan, what happened exactly?" He didn't seem to understand himself, but just remembering how he had felt started to affect him again.

Once we walked in the doors at home he said he would be in his room and asked not to be bothered. We told him Bethany was going to come by and try to help us sort everything out and help him feel better. We also said we were praying for him and we were hurting because he was hurting. We wanted him to know we were for him, not against him, and we felt the gravity of his pain. We wanted him to know, without a doubt, he wasn't alone in his hurt.

We could hear him sobbing through the door as he shut it and then threw himself onto his bed. He tried to muffle the sound of his cries by putting a pillow over him, but we could still hear the anguish of his grief in those moments. Our hearts were breaking for this boy whom we loved so dearly. It hurt profoundly to know he was in so much pain but not know what to do to help him.

Bethany arrived and walked back to his room to talk with him. We noticed many times it was easier for Jonathan to talk to a third-party involved because he didn't have to worry about hurting Michael and my feelings if he were talking about his biological parents. He continued to struggle with perceived loyalties. He thought we were against each other (foster parents versus biological parents), but ultimately we were on the same team. We all wanted what was best for the children.

As much as we loved Jonathan and wanted to adopt him, we understood the deep love and affection he held for his biological parents. We would never want to take that away or diminish it. They gave him life and despite their struggles in life right now, they loved him profoundly.

Bethany walked out of Jonathan's room to update us about the seriousness of the situation. I knew by the look on her face, before she even said a word, everything was not okay.

"Jonathan is feeling overwhelmed with everything going on," she whispered to us. "It's like the feelings inside of him are in constant battle. I don't want you to be scared, but you need to know Jonathan is considering harming himself to try to feel better or at least make it all end. I don't think he would actually harm himself, but he needs to know we are going to take his words seriously."

That night Jonathan had to be assessed by our local Acute Child Psychiatry Service to be sure he was safe in our home and wasn't going to harm himself.

I had to breathe. The air inside of my chest was being sucked out of me, and I couldn't take a breath in those moments immediately following Bethany's words. I escaped to our backyard and started pacing up and down the driveway. Tears came heavy.

Michael and Bethany spoke a little while longer inside, then Bethany had to make a few phone calls. I paced back and forth over the hard, cold pavement without a jacket yet oblivious to the cold November day. I simply focused on trying to get a hold of myself. The hair on my arms were sticking up from the cold, but I was sweating from the chaos going on inside of me.

After a while, Bethany came out to check on me. "Are you okay?" she asked calmly.

"It hurts me so deeply to know how he is hurting right now," I said, not knowing any other way to describe how deeply grieved I felt in those moments over Jonathan's pain.

Bethany went on to say she was amazed at how much love Jonathan was receiving from us, even though he had no idea. She explained how she knew from our reaction the depth of our love for this boy. Tears started coming as I realized how very true her words were. The hurt I was feeling in those moments was because my heart felt such affection for Jonathan. Physical birth pangs signify you're a mother, but the heart pangs of raising children signify you're a mom. In those moments, I felt like Jonathan's mom.

Children in foster care face seemingly insurmountable obstacles every day. They have to overcome the stereotypes and stigmas as well as the personal struggles in their own heart. That doesn't even include overcoming generational sin patterns carried from one generation to the next simply by habit and not knowing another way. It sometimes feels impossible to break the cycle of brokenness these children face.

Praise God He is in the business of proclaiming beauty and purpose in the pain and brokenness of life. He redeems. He stays with us in the midst of our mess and heartache and struggle, and never leaves us. He feels our pain and He draws us into His presence. He takes every piece of our life and strings it together to make a masterpiece that declares His Love over His people. God is Sovereign over all. Although it was one of the darkest days of our journey, we received a glimmer of hope before we went to bed.

During the assessment Jonathan finally talked about some of the feelings he had been burying deep inside. He was letting a burden off of his shoulder and talking about how he felt in more specific ways than he had previously.

As long as we keep silent about struggles and feelings, the enemy of our soul will use it to torture us from the inside out. It's only when we bring these distorted truths into the light of God's Word and share honestly with others that we can begin to see progress. Jonathan was beginning to open up and allow others to share in his grief, this alone would help him to begin moving forward.

After the evaluator talked with Jonathan she briefly talked to me. I was surprised at the change in tone, she spoke peacefully. She pulled me aside and said, "Jonathan talked very clearly about his thoughts to hurt himself, even to the point of having a plan. However, he doesn't seem to actually want to end his life. He simply wants to feel some kind of control and a feeling other than confusion and being lost in a world where he can't quite find his bearings."

According to her, he seemed to be sorting through his feelings in an age-appropriate way and did not give her cause for concern. She was amazed at his confidence in our love for him and desire for him to feel safe and wanted. This confidence was in fact causing the most struggle in his heart. He hadn't expected to want to stay in a foster home, but he wanted to stay with us forever.

NOT-SO-HAPPY HOLIDAYS

Once Jonathan broke the silence about many of his feelings, Jazmine started to follow suit, although on a more surface-level degree, which given her age, almost six years old, made perfect sense. This lengthened our difficult season, but became a period of great progress. The kids were beginning to talk about the hurt their biological parents had caused them and about how they felt being removed from everything they once knew. They weren't hiding their emotional state from us as much anymore.

Fits and tantrums were all the more abundant and extreme, but now we were able to follow-up occurrences with intentional conversations. Although we didn't see much decrease in intensity or frequency of fits, the conversations were meaningful. We took great hope in knowing no season lasts forever and one day, we prayed soon, the children's emotions would be more stable and controlled. This change would come as long as we continued to be patient, consistent, and loved them no matter their behaviors. They needed to know our love for them was unconditional. They needed to learn what real love was.

Many kids coming from hard backgrounds have to learn this because real love isn't our culture's standard. In the world, and often in the homes these kids come from, love is based on action. If children don't perform a certain way, love is withheld. The love we were trying to show the children was the same unconditional and never-ending love Christ calls us to show others, and shows us Himself. We were trying to live out 1 Corinthians 13 to them:

> "Love is patient and kind; love does not envy or boast; it is not arrogant or rude. It does not insist on its own way; it is not irritable or resentful; it does not rejoice at wrongdoing, but rejoices with the truth. Love bears all things, believes all things, hopes all things, endures all things. Love never ends."[6]

Never were we perfect in loving the children, but even our imperfect love made a difference in their hearts.

We had been warned the first holiday season in foster care was one of the hardest times for children to get through. They

---

[6] 1 Corinthians 13:4-8

knew the holidays were supposed to be a happy time, and they may even have happy memories from their biological family. However, for foster children, the holidays are generally a near-constant reminder that they have been removed from their biological family. They are grieving the loss of everything that used to be, all over again. It can be even more difficult when foster children experience happiness at their foster home, because it again causes a struggle with assumed loyalties in a child's heart and creates the inner turmoil that then overflows into out-of-control behaviors.

Our kids were not exempt from a difficult holiday season. Like I shared at the beginning of this chapter, the difficult days started around the middle of October and, unfortunately, continued until just after Christmas. During these months a day did not pass when we weren't dealing with major fits, tantrums, and situations which caused chaos in our home, family, and hearts. There was lots of screaming, yelling, and anger being thrown our way. We juggled as best we could.

I remember in our training to be licensed as foster parents our workers talked about vicarious trauma. We are hearing about and learning from these children the deep neglect and abuse they suffered. Simply by hearing and witnessing their behavior that comes from their trauma, we are affected by the knowledge and exposure. Common signs and symptoms are withdrawing socially, mood swings, sensitivity, and difficulty sleeping (to name a few). Vicarious trauma can often lead to burnout unless appropriate preventative actions are taken. The best way to combat vicarious trauma and burnout is by effectively using self-care techniques.

Once behaviors started escalating we couldn't keep up with our self-care. We needed two adults at home as much as possible. Additionally, we were often too tired to do anything proactive for our own selves. We wondered if we would get through.

Sometimes at night Michael and I would lay in bed exhausted and, though knowing with full confidence we were doing exactly what we were supposed to do, we would have doubts because the issues were multiplying and we didn't know what to do.

"Are we going to make it?" Michael would ask me. With tears of exhaustion and desperation I would reply, "I don't know. It doesn't feel like it. But they need us, so we have to try."

There was no amount of training that could have prepared us for what we were going through. I think there is just a part of actually living a situation that makes it real. You can't fabricate everything that you are going to experience and feel in a training environment or reading material. Part of that simply comes from living.

It helped greatly to connect with other foster and adoptive

parents. It helped us to know people who had survived the tumultuous season of foster care and difficult child behaviors. It gave us at least a little bit of confidence that we would probably survive too.

Despite this truth and slight hope, we were still right in the midst of it all, living each day in chaos. The house was a mess, the kids were a mess, and Michael and I were a mess too.

A few days before Christmas we were told Madison had checked herself into rehab. In the moments following this news my world felt like it was crumbling around me. I lost my breath and felt as if I was grasping for air, for security, for anything that would make me feel okay. Life felt comfortable with the children, despite the hard situations we faced. We loved these kids and wanted them to stay with us forever and be adopted into our family.

Despite the struggles, life still felt normal and I felt deep love for these children. I often forgot the truth that my title of mother only came with the word foster before it. This news of potential progress brought me back to reality, reminding me adoption was not guaranteed. At any time Madison and Aaron could start working on their goals and begin working toward reunification. This news made it difficult to stay in the moment during the next few days and celebrate Christmas, especially when tantrums were still abundant and Michael and I were exhausted beyond anything we'd ever experienced.

MARRIAGE WOES

After hearing the news of Madison being in rehab, I struggled to focus on anything and was even more emotional than normal. Just a few days after Christmas, once the dust started to settle from the chaos of the previous three months and after all the kids were in bed, Michael and I got into a huge fight. I don't even remember how it started. I said he wasn't doing enough. He said I expected too much out of him. I said he was lazy. He said I loved the children more than him.

We were both exhausted and weary and worn out. We both said words we didn't mean. We had been living in such a difficult time. We were fighting against each other, instead of remembering we were allies.

Because we could only leave the children with people who had their fingerprints on record with our state worker, we had only been on one date since the children joined our home. We were also missing out on daily meaningful interactions because we would fall asleep minutes after the children at night. We hardly had time or energy for intimacy. We were living from one thing to the next, constantly going and never resting or finding refreshment. We were in survival mode in our family, home, marriage, and own hearts.

Michael and I were both doing the best we could, unfortunately with everything we were facing in life, our best wasn't good enough.

We realized that evening, through our fight, we had been giving everything we had to the children and making sure they were taken care of and following all the rules and keeping all the necessary appointments. We didn't have any time to take care of ourselves, let alone pour into each other. We had let our marriage fall to the side amidst the chaos.

Not only that, but seeing all the struggles in the children's lives was affecting us both and we weren't talking about it. We weren't talking about how our childhoods had been difficult and we were remembering more as the children were sharing about their life. We weren't talking about the fact it was truly hard to care for these children at times. Their needs were so great and they required so much out of us, nearly everything we had. We weren't talking about how we truly, truly doubted whether we would get through this season in one piece. In the weariness of the days our faith and marriage were being tested.

We needed to remember we were there for each other. Our marriage and relationship had great purpose in the midst of all this chaos. Not only that, but Christ was with us through it all. He had never left our side.

MILESTONES IN THE MIDST OF CHAOS

I have already mentioned Michael and I hadn't expected to parent an infant. Therefore, the milestones with Kyle and

Christina were all the more special because we never thought we would get to experience them.

During the tumultuous months leading up to Christmas, there were a few beautiful, glorious moments of motherhood as I watched the little kids continue to develop and thrive. A couple of the milestones stand out.

In the middle of November, Kyle said his first word. He looked at me with big beautiful blue eyes and smiled as wide as he could and said, "Momma." Hearing the big kids call me "Mom" for the first time was incredibly special, and it was just as special when Kyle said it.

Being so young and not knowing what was going on, Christina didn't know us as anything but mom and dad. When she came to us at thirteen-months-old, she was completely non-verbal except for her screaming. We quickly started working with her to teach her baby sign language to help minimize her frustration at not being able to communicate with us. She had never attempted to call us "Ms. Ashley" or "Mr. Michael." However, I remember in the fall her starting to use the name "Daddy" when talking to or about Michael.

A couple of weeks after Kyle started saying momma, Christina said it for the first time too. It brought me to tears. Christina had been such a difficult child and caring for her took so much energy from me. She looked straight at me and said,

"Momma." Hearing her voice call out to me was such a beautiful sound. In that moment, "Momma" was more than a label. It was as if she was saying she belonged to me, knew I loved her, and claimed me as her mom.

Despite the hard days we faced in the winter months, there were still many moments that gave us great hope for our future. That is love made real.

There were many times as we pursued adopting the children that I realized in a fresh way the significance of my salvation and adoption into God's family. He pursued me. He loved me despite my sinfulness and failures. Just as it says in Galatians, He came to redeem us so that we may receive adoption as sons and cry out, "Abba! Father!" to the One who saved us and welcomed us into His family forever[7].

---

[7] Galatians 4:4-7

The Limbo Life
Chapter Eight

As 2013 began we were excited and hopeful life would start to calm down. January brought days that felt completely normal. The fits and outbursts were decreasing. Jonathan only had temper issues about three times a week. Jazmine was down from multiple tantrums a day to only five or six fits a week. Christina was still struggling with her tantrums, but even she had shown improvement. She had gone from ten fits a day to only five.

Michael and I were beginning to feel more rested and we felt hopeful as we waited to hear a TPR date. January welcomed us with arms wide open and gave us an opportunity to take a nice, long, deep breath.

In late-January Kyle started saying "Daddy." Of course, Michael was thrilled with this new skill. It was an exciting time as we watched him learn to do new things, like crawl and babble more. There was one small problem though: When he started saying "Daddy," he stopped saying "Momma."

I know he didn't stop saying "Momma" on purpose, but I was still hurt when he stopped. Up until that point, he would say "Momma" often. He'd look up at me throughout the day and say the beautiful word which meant I belonged to him and he was mine. I told myself not to worry about this small issue, perhaps Kyle was just fixated on his new word.

As we waited on our TPR date, Terri, our state worker, was so kind and patient with me. I would call once a week, at least, to check in and make sure she hadn't heard anything about a date. I wanted to be sure our case was fresh on her mind. Plus I enjoyed encouraging her in her job as well. Sometimes I would call on the weekend just to leave a message that she would get first thing on Monday letting her know I was praying for her. I also sent pictures of the children to Terri and Angela, our agency worker, so they could get a peek into our daily lives. I cannot imagine the stress that comes with the job of a social worker. Because of this, I wanted to do my best to encourage our workers while I had a direct line to them.

One day in February, Terri called with the wonderful news.

"We have our TPR date!" she said with excitement in her voice. "The pre-trial will be held in April."

I didn't understand, though. What did she mean "pre-trial" date? I hadn't known we would have a pre-trial, and I didn't know what a pre-trial even was.

"A pre-trial date will serve as an opportunity for Madison and Aaron to voluntarily terminate their parental rights before having to move on to a trial," Terri explained. "If they don't show up or if they do not voluntarily terminate their parental rights, then the court will assign us a trial date."

Because the court date was in April (one year since the kids entering state's care), we would also have our annual review of the case at the same time.

Hearing this news was discouraging. I had hoped to adopt the kids in the summer and had already started a Pinterest board for the adoption celebration carnival I had been thinking about. Now we wouldn't even have a pre-trial until April; followed by a trial date. Then we would have to wait through appeal periods and paperwork processes before getting an adoption date. I asked a few more questions about why we had to have a pre-trial and why it seemed to be so far away. I know Terri could sense my disappointment.

I was trying to hold it together but tears were already streaming down my face as I tried to end our phone call. Before hanging up Terri gently reminded me to keep my perspective.

"Ashley, these things take time and we have to follow the process," she assured me. "Things are moving forward, focus on that."

In the moments after I hung up the phone I felt like the world was crashing around me and I couldn't keep steady. Standing on the front porch, I let the news sink in. I took a seat on our front steps and buried my face in my hands as my tears fell to the ground, all while the babies napped inside.

I was ready for the limbo to end. Yet in reality it was just beginning. This realization altered my expectations of when we would adopt the kids. It seemed so far away. I wondered if I would be strong enough to keep going when all I wanted was to give these precious children, and really myself, the confidence that would come with adoption.

In the weeks after receiving our pre-trial date, I was extremely sensitive. Anything could spark an emotional response. The kids would remind me of their wish to stay with us forever, and tears would come. All I wanted to do was shout, "YES! You can rest in the safety of our love now and forever." But I couldn't, because there was no security for any of us.

Once the tears started to come it was hard to turn them off again. There were many nights after getting the kids in bed that I spent in tears, questioning if we'd get to adopt them and how long we'd have to wait.

I loved these children with everything in me and I wanted them to stay with us forever. Yet with this added time I was terrified Madison and Aaron would start fighting and working on their court orders and change everything. I had heard stories of biological parents making improvements right at the end, which lengthened the process by months, even years, simply by showing a little progress at just the right time.

I never felt safe. I tried my best to be present and in the moment with the children, but in reality I was terrified my life was a ticking time bomb and had a countdown for when this dream would explode in pieces around me.

Michael would often hold me as I cried myself to sleep at night. He would whisper to me encouraging words, "It's going to be okay. It's just a few more months."

He has always had lower expectations than me in situations like our adoption. Lower expectations mean less disappointment. He so easily trusted if these children were meant to be ours then the Lord would take care of the details. He would remind me repeatedly on especially emotional days, "This is not outside of God's control."

It was during this time I started to bear the burden of our children's case more. I began to feel as if I were responsible for making sure our workers were doing everything as quickly as possible. I called asking about progress and hoping to keep our case in the front of everyone's mind. Despite the setback in my ideal timeline, I was willing to do anything I could to keep our case moving toward adoption, and as quickly as possible. Once the adoption was finalized I believed life would really start to settle down and the kids would be even more confident in their place in our family. Then I would be able to relax and breathe again.

At the time, I struggled to remember the truth that my plans don't always match God's plans. I had wanted to become a mom for many years before I met these children. Yet, had I had become a mother then, I wouldn't have them. When I look back, I see God's hand and His faithfulness and the reality that His plan truly is good. Even so, I forgot God's timeline was sometimes different than mine and His timeline alone would ultimately bring Him the most glory.

TELLING THE KIDS

The big kids were starting to ask more often about staying with us forever and being adopted. After talking with Bethany, our main therapist, we decided it was okay to tell the kids. We believed the children knowing our desire to adopt them would bring them comfort. Michael and I also thought knowing this would help them realize even if they didn't return to their biological parents that we would fight for them to stay with us, if necessary.

The next time Jazmine or Jonathan asked about staying with us forever, we would tell them we hoped they would be able to. We would also share with them our desire to adopt them.

A few days after making this decision, Jonathan was giving me a hug on his way to bed and said, "I love you, Mom. I hope you are my mom forever."

As I stood in the hallway of our cozy house I looked him in his eyes, Jazmine was standing right there too, and said, "Me too buddy. I hope I get to be your mom forever and adopt you so that you will always know I am your mom and I love you. That would make me so happy!" Both of the big kids smiled and I pulled them in close kissing their heads as I smiled with them and happy tears rolled down my cheek.

Being able to tell Jonathan and Jazmine we wanted to adopt them was such a relief, for them and us. I finally felt like they better understood our heart toward them. Not only that, but Jonathan seemed to be more confident in his place in our family after we declared to him we wanted him and would fight for him. Around the same time, we were excited to be moving into a bigger house that would be a more permanent and spacious home for us all. The kids were thrilled once we found our new house and started making plans for our big move.

ROUGH WATERS AHEAD

Before spring break, which was also a couple of weeks before we moved, we entered another difficult season full of out-of-control behavior. This season would last much longer and was more intense than the previous one in the early-winter months. We had no down time because we were handling crisis after crisis.

Jazmine's behavior struggles came back and were more intense than before. Her problems at school were daily and she was removed from her classroom many times each day. She was sent home early from school several times and even suspended from school during testing week. I assume it was because she was a distraction to her peers who needed to focus in a quiet and controlled environment, of which she could not contribute to.

Her behaviors often carried over into the evening. There were many days when she was in and out of time out and sent to bed early. Because she was so full of energy, she was unable to be out of our sight during this time. Her erratic behavior also started taking place outside of school and home. We were unable to attend church regularly during this time, and even trying to grab dinner out was a difficult task.

Many times her fits were completely unrestrained and she only calmed down after screaming, kicking, and wailing for a time. Just getting it out seemed like the only option. Her fits were exaggerated when she had an audience. We would send her to her room until she could calm down. I'd tell her, "Jazmine, this is not acceptable. If you are going to continue throwing a fit, you need to do so in your room." Rarely would she choose to stop. Screaming and stomping the whole time, she would make it to her bedroom and stay there until the fit was done. Most times she would walk to her room herself, but sometimes we would have to carry her. Whenever we had to interact with her during a fit, her aggression would often turn to us. Michael and I often received mild injuries once we arrived to her room.

A few weeks after our move Bethany mentioned to us that she believed the move might have triggered Jazmine's behavior. In Jazmine's subconscious mind (with her mild attachment struggles), she could have been worried our moving meant she wasn't moving with us or that we were leaving her. It also could have reminded her of her life before she came to us, because they moved often and without warning. Because of her history, it seemed our move created an unstable environment which caused much chaos in the depths of her heart.

Jonathan's struggles during this time were less violent and more internal and verbal. He had angry tendencies which became more visible when he didn't get his way. Often times hearing the word "no" would cause a screaming fit with disrespectful dialogue, generally targeted at me, and then he would be sent to his room to settle down. Once in his room, he would punch his pillow, or scream into it to get out the aggression. His fits were much less frequent than Jazmine's. For that I was happy.

I remember during this time visiting with my friend Indy during rest time, which was the respite in my day when the kids were all in their rooms sleeping or relaxing with a book. Yes, I made all four children take a "rest time" when they were home. This was a key to my sanity. I needed that time in the middle of the day to get through. Most days I would nap, occasionally I would read a book, other times I would catch up on a podcast or listen to a sermon. This time also gave Jazmine and Jonathan time away from each other, which they needed.

Indy was helping me organize one of our rooms at the new house and asked how I was doing. Instead of just smiling and saying fine, I spoke to her heart-to-heart. We sat on the floor unpacking books and placing them on nearby bookshelves while I cried hot tears and talked honestly about how hard life was. I shared how the kids were struggling and having many behavior problems. I expressed to her my hurt as I saw the kids struggling.

Indy hugged me as we cried together on the floor surrounded with now-empty boxes.

"Although life is much harder than you thought it would be, I know the Lord is with you and will never leave you, especially during this hard season," she said.

Indy reminded of the beautiful truth that the Lord never leaves or forsakes us, just like the promise made to the Israelites[8]. He had called me to this life and these children and He was right there with me each day helping me get through by His grace.

Despite the fact we didn't tell the children about court dates and important case meetings, I believe they could sense the anxiety in the house as we neared our pre-trial. It could have been the cause for much of the chaos they felt. I tried my best to hide my anxieties, but I know I didn't succeed. I'm sure they felt the tension.

With April finally came our pre-trial and nothing changed, except now we had a trial date for August. At the time, August felt like years away in my mind. We were dealing with constant ups and downs at home and the kids needed to know they were going to be with us. They needed the stability and confidence adoption would bring, and honestly, I craved it as well.

I cried out to God and prayed, "Lord, please let this summer pass by quickly and give me unimaginable peace as we wait for this season to end. I'm growing so weary. Help me finish this race strong, by Your power and grace."

As summer 2013 began Jonathan's behaviors started to settle out. He was talking more instead of yelling and working on not bottling up his feelings. It was a beautiful transformation to

---

[8] Deuteronomy 31:6

watch my angry son open up and start to loosen his grip on the feelings which often held him captive. He was starting to process his hurt again and the processing helped him be able to handle the disappointment that would come his way, especially when told "no."

Jazmine continued to struggle and that summer she was diagnosed with off-the-charts Attention Deficit Hyperactivity Disorder (ADHD) as well as Oppositional Defiant Disorder (ODD). We saw a child physiatrist who wanted to medicate Jazmine, however the state did not want her to be medicated. I didn't necessarily want to medicate her either (I always said I wouldn't), but I did want a solution to her behavior struggles before school started again. Michael and I started implementing The Feingold Diet and had great success. This is a diet program that eliminates artificial colors, flavors, sweeteners, and preservatives[9]. Toward the end of summer, Jazmine was having less than five episodes a week.

Michael and I were exhausted and weary throughout the summer. But I was reminded frequently, as Jonathan opened up more and Jazmine's fits became less frequent, that God was at work in our family even when I felt like everything was falling apart. So often He uses the inadequate to do His work, and that summer was full of Him pushing us forward, little by little. I did my best stay confident and prayed God would take our pain and redeem it for His great purposes.

---

[9] You can learn more here: http://www.feingold.org/

I believe everything in life happens for God's great overarching purpose and for His glory. I trust in the words of Romans 8:28, "And we know that for those who love God all things work together for good, for those who are called according to his purpose." It might not be for our immediate happiness, but God has a purpose for all things.

A NEW AWARENESS

Michael and I soon realized we would be struggling with some behaviors and adjustments with the children, specifically the big kids, for a long time. Even if we adopted the kids, it wouldn't erase everything they've been through. Being adopted and in foster care will always be a part of who they are. Throughout their lives, young and old, struggles will come up as they realize anew everything that happened. They will have new questions for us the older they get and will understand old answers in a different way.

According to the world's standards, we may never be a "normal" family. We will always be affected by this experience and have our quirks which will make us stand out and be unique as a unit and as individuals.

Philip, an elder of our church, was at our house one day during the summer. He had begun studying with Jonathan what it meant to be a follower of Christ. On this particular day, as he prepared to leave our house, he must have noticed I was heavy-burdened. Philip asked me a powerful question that can hold much value when answered with honesty and vulnerability, "How are you doing?"

Instead of replying with the easy answer of "I'm okay," I shared through tears, "I'm struggling to adjust some of my ideas of what our family will look like long-term. It isn't everything I imagined it would be. Some days, it is just so hard."

When we chose to adopt through foster care, Michael and I understood the children would have more of a history than if we adopted an infant. However, does God turn us away when we call out to Him despite the various ways we have failed Him or fallen short of His expectations? Does God turn people away because they have baggage from their past life experiences? *No!* How could we overlook children simply because they had lived a hard life and would be affected by their history?

I trusted the Lord brought these amazing children into my life because He had called me, specifically, to love them and parent them. I was chosen to be their mom. They were chosen to be my children. They might not be everything I imagined, in many ways they are so much more. Yet I needed to adjust my expectations. I couldn't change them. I simply needed to love them for who they were.

I always wanted to homeschool our children. In high school I watched with great interest several families in our church who homeschooled their children. I especially enjoyed watching the close family bonds that came as a result of this educational choice. I valued the idea of teaching my children at home and being able to spend more time with them and cater their education to their specific needs. Shortly after this new awareness of our family, I began wanting to homeschool even more.

Jazmine struggled so much in kindergarten, I was worried about her being pushed into first grade unprepared. The public school system wouldn't allow her to repeat kindergarten because of a district-wide policy, despite Terri, our state worker, supporting the decision. Jonathan was doing fine academically, but socially he was going to be entering a difficult season when peer pressure can be hard to fight. Additionally, we wanted the children home with us so we could do our best to intentionally pour into their lives, directly shape their character, and give them a Biblical worldview.

After talking to our agency director about homeschooling, we learned the state can give foster families permission to homeschool in special circumstances. Michael and I had assumed we would not be able to make this change until we adopted. This new discovery gave us a little hope that we could bring the kids home for school. We asked Terri if she could try and get us the needed special permission to homeschool the children in the fall.

Unfortunately, she could not get us the permission.

"The state is very strict about giving this permission," Terri said the day she called me with the news. "I'm sorry, I just couldn't get it approved."

She did tell us, however, we could enroll the kids in private school. We found a small private school in which we believed the children would thrive. Jazmine would also be able to repeat kindergarten and learn many of the things she missed because of her struggles the previous year.

WE SIGNED UP FOR THIS

We were beyond exhausted as summer came to an end. Not only that, but Michael and I were still struggling to find the time to build each other up and cultivate our marriage in the midst of the chaos. We had worked hard to pour into the children and we needed to start balancing parenting and marriage. We needed to get back into a healthy and thriving marriage that would set the tone for the whole house.

We signed up for this life. Not only that, but we were committed to each other until death. We were in this for the long haul, with the children and each other. It was so much harder than we had ever thought it would be. But you know what? We wouldn't change a thing.

We wanted to be parents and this is the way God chose to bring us children. Our commitment to these kids was a promise we lived every day with our love and care. I fully agree with what Jen Hatmaker said in a blog post after bringing her two children home from Africa[10],

> "You cannot just be into *adoption* to adopt; you have to be into *parenting*. And it is hard, hard, intentional, laborious work. Children who have been abused, abandoned, neglected, given away, given up, and left alone are shaken so deeply, so intrinsically, they absolutely require parents who are willing to wholly invest in their healing; through the screaming, the fits, the anger, the shame, the entitlement, the bed-wetting, the spitting, the rejection, the bone-chilling fear."

We signed up for this life and we are committed to these children, with joy, and for whatever comes our way. We were committed the moment we met them. These were *our* kids. Even more so, we believed the Lord was the One who orchestrated all this and brought them into our life. He would guide us and give us the strength to get through the difficult seasons. We found great hope in this reminder, and trusted He would never leave us or forsake us on this journey, no matter how dark it got.

---

[10] Hatmaker, Jen. "After the Airport." *JenHatmaker.com*. n.p., 6 September 2011. Web. 5 October 2014.

It didn't make it easier, but it gave us great hope and purpose. There is no guarantee life is going to go the way you always dreamed it would. I had wanted to be a mother for as long as I could remember. Yet, the process was so incredibly difficult. Life is beautiful and wonderful, but oh so hard at the same time.

Final Farewells
Chapter Nine

As we got closer to our TPR trial date Terri mentioned a final visit. *Hold on...what?!?* The moment she said "final visit" my stomach jumped inside of me and I immediately felt like I was going to throw up my lunch. The children hadn't seen their parents since being placed in state's care, except for the one visit with Aaron, which never should have happened. We were going on sixteen months of no contact and great progress in adjusting and expressing feelings. Now we had to have a visit? Yet again I was facing the unknown of what would happen and what it would mean for our kids and their slowly growing sense of security.

"Do we have to have a final visit?" I asked in desperation.

"If the children's therapist is against the visit then we might not have to have one," Terri said. "Otherwise it's required by law if the biological parents request one."

I immediately called Bethany and asked her to consider

whether she thought a final visit was in the best interest of the children.

We waited a couple of days for an answer. The entire time we were waiting there were worst-case scenarios going through my head. *What if their biological parents talk poorly about us or told the kids not to accept us as their parents? What if they decide to try to hurt Michael or me? What if they followed us home? What if the kids, unknowingly, shared information that jeopardizes the safety of our family?*

When Bethany called me back, she said most people at our agency, including herself, were in favor of a final visit. I started crying, the ugly cry. In that moment I couldn't imagine any good coming from a visit. We had made so much progress during the summer, were so close to the trial, and anticipated moving on with adoption. Putting them in a situation that could trigger behaviors and emotions the big kids had been working hard to overcome broke my heart. Yet, Bethany stressed she believed the children, especially Jonathan, would benefit from the closure. She also believed because of the progress they had made and the assurance and security they receive from us they would be able to process the visit and move on with little to no backlash.

ANSWERED PRAYERS AND A QUICK TRIAL
On the morning of August 15th, we told the children we were

going to court and what they could expect while we were there. They seemed excited, yet also nervous about this change. Jonathan understood more of what was happening and realized the next step was adoption. Even though thinking about adoption was exciting for him, processing the finalization of never returning to his biological parents was difficult. As I looked him in his eyes and then hugged him goodbye, I could tell he was once again feeling conflicted as we moved forward.

In the days leading up to court, Jazmine and Jonathan had nightmares of Michael and I being killed and them being left alone. This terrified Jazmine, who would wake up crying in the middle of the night. There were also more frequent nighttime bathroom issues. We believe these issues were due to their nerves and the stress of the situation.

As Michael and I drove to the courthouse on that August morning that would change our lives, we had no idea what to expect. We knew at the end the biological parent's rights would, more than likely, be terminated. We weren't confident in the way this change would happen. Either the judge would cause the change or the biological parents would voluntarily terminate their rights.

We were thankful the day had finally come when we would begin to feel security, or at least we hoped we would. We often prayed for the Lord to allow everyone involved to consider what was best for the children. We were more than ready for the bumpy roads of foster care to come to an end. We wanted to rest in the knowledge we were a family, once and for all and for forever. This was a step toward the dream of adoption.

Aaron was in jail at the time, but he was able to appear in court. We were concerned about Madison getting there, logistically, but she made it. She seemed on edge and looked far worse than the last time I had seen her. Each time I saw her she seemed to visibly age by years. Thinking of the powers against her because of addiction made me sad.

Madison no longer had control over her life. The addiction controlled her. Even the help that had been offered wasn't enough to guide her toward recovery, despite the risk of losing her kids. I had never in my life seen addiction destroy a person's life like this. The events that led to our children's adoption grieve me deeply, the depravity of a life held captive by addiction is sickening. Every adoption starts with loss, grief, and sadness. As sweet as the day was, in terms of progress towards adoption, it held so much bitterness.

Our case was called and we sat in the courtroom and watched in sadness, as well as a sense of awe, as one by one parental rights were *voluntarily* terminated. Even Jonathan's biological father, who was phoned in from prison in another state, voluntarily terminated his rights. I'm sure it wasn't an easy decision for them, but I do believe they understood there was no reason to fight. As difficult as it was, they had already missed their chance to get the children back.

Michael and I watched Madison and Aaron ten feet from us. In anguish and despair, they gave up their children. They said the children were better off somewhere else, without them. Their hearts seemed heavy as they cried and, I can only assume, debated in their mind the reality of what they were doing.

Not only did they voluntarily terminate their parental rights one by one, but they also made known their desires for the children to stay with us and be adopted. My heart was utterly conflicted during those moments. I never take for granted the fact they experienced such great loss as I tuck my children in each night.

We were done with court within thirty minutes. Although we were excited about moving forward toward adoption, our hearts were burdened by the events in the courtroom. We arrived home to share the news. We told the children their biological parents had, by their own choices, terminated their rights and in doing so gave us their permission to move forward with adoption.

Jonathan smiled at first, but then seemed to understand what this decision meant at a deeper level and tears quickly formed in his eyes.

"They didn't even try," he cried. Deep down he wanted to

know they had put up a fight. He wanted to know he was worth the pain it would take to at least try to get them back. Watching him process this hurt was heartbreaking.

As much as we could, Michael and I explained how addiction creates a different person. I pulled Jonathan aside to explain in more detail.

"The people in court were not the same people you remember," I told him. "Their lives have been altered so drastically because of drugs. I'm so sorry sweetie."

Unfortunately, they simply weren't able to make the hard choices they would have had to make to parent the kids. Jonathan understood these truths, yet the pain still lingered. It showed on his face. I held him close as I felt the wetness from his tears on my shoulder, a heart broken.

A FINAL VISIT

The next week Terri mentioned she was going to do her best to arrange the final visit before our case was transferred to the adoption department. She was going to set it for one hour and it would be finished when the ending time came, whether or not the biological parents were on time in the beginning. She also wanted to make sure Michael and I were in the room, as well as Grandma Susie, Bethany, and herself. We also had the children's aunt and uncle present. We all wanted to be sure the children's safety and emotional security were carefully watched over during the visit.

Knowing there would be so many adults present who had the children's best interest at heart, made me feel more confident that everything would be okay. But I was still nervous all the same. I couldn't eat anything the entire day. I was so anxious and worried about what was going to happen. Michael and I had discussed with Bethany what to expect and how to talk to the children about the visit. She made it a point to tell us during the visit our role was strictly to observe and offer emotional support for the children. She advised us against intervening for behavior problems or anything inappropriate, either she or Terri would handle those situations.

In the days approaching the visit, we asked the children what would make them most comfortable during the visit. Jazmine had said she wanted to be able to play and talk. Jonathan said he would like pizza or a meal.

"Because that's what family does, they eat together," Jonathan said. I replied back to him, "Well, we could bring some snacks, will that be okay?" Jonathan quickly answered, "Yes. Can there be some cookies?"

The visit was going to happen in the waiting area of Terri's office. It was after normal business hours, so there wouldn't be anyone else there. We would have lots of seating options and some open space as well. We also learned that Aaron was out of jail now, so both Madison and Aaron would be at the visit.

On the way to the meeting, we asked the children if they had any questions. We did our best to speak positively about what was going to happen. Bethany had mentioned, although we weren't actively involved in the visit, we would set the tone for them leading up to, during, and after the visit. The children would take cues from us about how to feel. Therefore, we wanted to be sure we made the children as comfortable as possible. We also had a list of things we were supposed to be sure they knew they weren't to mention, like the name of their school, or our address and phone number.

We unloaded the children and the snacks and went into the building to wait. The big kids were standing at the door, their eyes locked on the parking lot, watching for any cars to pull in. We had assumed Madison and Aaron would show up, but as the time started to pass we wondered if they had decided not to come. However, about fifteen minutes later they arrived. I didn't mind the waiting too much because it meant the visit would be shorter. I was a nervous wreck as they walked toward the door. My hands were shaking and I was very hot.

Jonathan had been nervous leading up to the visit and I didn't know how he was going to react. All week he had been saying to me, "I'm going to yell. I'm going to let them know that I am angry at them and tell them that they chose drugs over me." I replied to him with a soft tone, trying to help him consider another option, "Jonathan, I know that you are so angry. So am I! None of this is right. But this is the last time you are going to see each other for a long time. Is that how you want them to remember you? Not only that, but is that how you want to remember your last time together?"

When the moment came, he was just a boy and knew he wanted to be hugged. His love outweighed his anger.

Madison and Aaron came in and Jazmine and Jonathan ran straight to them giving hugs and kisses. I said hello and then quickly sat in a chair in the corner and watched as the meeting went on. The smiles were abundant and the love was clear.

Christina and Kyle didn't know what was going on. They just seemed to think there was a bunch of adults and play time. They played some and talked a little with Madison and Aaron. They came back to Michael and me often throughout the visit.

The time felt like it was going so slow, and afterward everyone said the same thing. A few times Terri and Bethany had to redirect children who were gravitating with guidance away from the group. But overall the visit wasn't anything like the horrible situation I had imagined it would be. The kids seemed to understand this was their time to play, laugh, have fun, and eventually say goodbye. Madison and Aaron seemed to understand the same. They weren't angry or mean-spirited, they were loving and affectionate to the kids and even went so far to confirm our role as their parents.

When it was time to leave there were tears all around. Madison and Aaron were crying. Jonathan was tearing up. Jazmine was more upset than anyone and just like during the one visit we had, I had to pull her away as she cried. We went into a back room where we waited for their biological parents to leave. The whole time we were waiting, Jazmine cried and screamed for her mommy and daddy. Once they left, Jonathan said he was ready to leave and seemed calm. Jazmine continued crying until we got outside. It was as if she thought they were going to be waiting for her. Yet, when she saw they had left, she seemed ready to continue on.

As we drove home we again asked if the kids had any questions. One of the questions Jonathan asked was, "Why did my mom look so different? Her face had lots of spots and she looked a lot older than I remember." Michael and I tried to answer as positively as we could. After we were done talking about the visit, they were both more quiet than normal. We knew this visit was going to be seared into their memories forever.

A WEEKEND AWAY

Part of the reason Michael and I wanted the final visit to happen when it did was because we had already planned a weekend trip with the big kids to the beach. We had hoped the timing would work well. We desired to transition from the final visit to our trip to allow more downtime than normal to process feelings and many opportunities to talk without the little kids also vying for our attention.

We arrived home and dropped Christina and Kyle off with my sister and mom who came down to spend time with them while we were with the big kids. As we finished the last-minute packing and loaded the van, I was overwhelmed with emotion as I told my sister how everything went. The visit had gone better than anyone could have expected. I was ashamed at how I had doubted the truth that the visit had been in God's control. He clearly had our family's future planned, and these were my sons and daughters. He wasn't going to allow an unexpected (to me) visit get in the way of everything we had been working toward with the children.

As we pulled away from our house, I could feel a small burden escaping me. Parental rights were terminated, the last visit had happened, now the case would be moving to the adoption department. Not only that, but we were told we would probably adopt in November, which meant we could go public just in time for National Adoption Awareness Month. Everything was coming together and the risk of losing the kids was becoming smaller.

The drive to the beach was quiet, I assume because there was much going on beneath the surface. We had left around eight o'clock in the evening and planned to drive through the night. The kids and I fell asleep as Michael drove. I took over driving for Michael around four in the morning so he could get some sleep. As everyone started rustling and the sun came up we stopped for breakfast. We were within an hour of reaching the shore.

As soon as I opened the door of the van, refreshing air overcame me, and all the tension that had become our life was swept away in the wind. During breakfast Michael and I took the opportunity to check in with the kids to see how they were feeling. I asked, "So, what did you think of the visit last night?"

"It was nice to see them again," Jazmine said with a smile. I thank God for how easy it was for her to just take everything at face value.

"I didn't get angry with them," Jonathan said with watery eyes. "I didn't ask why they had chosen drugs over me. I just wanted my last memory to be happy. And now we can move on and be a family." His wisdom never ceases to amaze me. He is wise beyond his years and experienced everything at such a deep understanding and grasp of what was going on.

We spent the next few days together letting the ocean wash away whatever pain and heartache we had. We laughed and played. The whole trip was therapeutic for us all. We spent meals together without the normal interruptions of Christina and Kyle, which helped us have meaningful conversations and appreciate Jazmine and Jonathan all the more. It was hard to be apart from the little kids, but deep down we knew the big kids needed us to be there fully for them.

Once we arrived back home, Jonathan began struggling more with his behavior, attitude, and anger. I believe he was still processing everything that was happening. We would talk often with him, and also let him call Grandma Susie to talk it through again with her. She was a great voice and influence for him because she has been there for him his whole life.

Just like before, this was something Jonathan would have to work through. There wasn't a way to get past it any quicker. We just loved him through the heartache and comforted him as best we could.

The Third Trimester of Foster Adoption
Chapter Ten

I anxiously awaited hearing from our new adoption state worker. Our paperwork had all been transferred to the adoption department. Michael and I were simply waiting to be introduced to the worker who would see our case through to the adoption finalization. As we neared the end of three weeks waiting, I started to get more anxious and wondered why we hadn't heard from our new worker yet. I e-mailed Tim, from our agency, and asked him to look into the delay for me. He replied within a day with our new worker's name, Lauren. He also said she had just been assigned to our case a few days prior and that he recommended waiting for her to reach out to us.

I do not do well waiting. It's the in-between times which make me most anxious. The times when I have done everything I am able to do and yet I am left resting in the hands of someone else, or waiting for something to happen. You would have thought I had become better at waiting, with all the waiting through infertility and the fostering process. Yet here I was again struggling through the pause.

The next week we heard from Lauren who proceeded to schedule a visit for the same week. I knew our case, and the speed of our adoption finalization, would rest in Lauren's hands. Because of this knowledge, the first visit was nerve-wrecking for me. I wanted this woman to see my deep love for these children, believe Michael and I were meant to be their parents, and work hard to make that happen in a courtroom quickly. We were ready for the law to catch up with our hearts.

THE WAITING

In September, we finished our first home visit with Lauren and I asked her how long she expected it would take to finalize our case. She said she generally gets cases through the process in sixty to ninety days.

"Are we on target to adopt in November then?" I asked her. Lauren replied, "I don't see November being a problem and it could even happen faster."

This was all the confirmation I needed. In my mind, we were going to adopt during November. There wasn't any other option, I needed a date. I needed to know it was going to happen and when. Lauren reminded me she wasn't giving me a guarantee, but I didn't accept that statement. It was going to happen in November and I was going to do everything in my power to make sure of it.

September and October weren't difficult to get through. I knew what we were working on. I knew we were headed to November and would adopt the kids. At our October home visit I asked Lauren, "Do you still think our adoption will be next month?" She said she was still hopeful, but again reminded me she wasn't guaranteeing a specific date. When I asked at the end of our visit about our November home visit, she said quickly, "Oh, we aren't scheduling one. If you adopt in November I won't need to come out." In my mind this was another confirmation of our November adoption.

The end of October came and November began. Early on I began to get worried. I assumed I would have heard something. I e-mailed Lauren within the first week of the month (I didn't want to seem too pushy by calling) to check in on the progress. She replied that she wanted to schedule a home visit. I didn't understand. I started crying the moment I saw the e-mail. Why did it seem like things were slowing down? I felt it deep in my heart. Suddenly I became worried that now, at the end, something was going to happen to delay the adoption or keep it from occurring altogether. This is honestly where my mind went.

I called Tim to ask him if he could try to check in with Lauren himself and see if there was something else going on that was causing the assumed delay. After we hung up the phone, I left to take the younger kids to story time like we had originally planned. This outing helped me not dwell on this new assumed realization.

As I was buckling the kids into their car seats after story time, Tim called me back.

"Hey Tim! Did you check into things for me?" I answered quickly.

"Ashley, you were right," Tim said. The world slowed down around me as I listened intently to his words.

"I was right?" I asked terrified. "What do you mean? What's going on?"

"Lauren seems concerned about you and Michael's discipline methods," he said hesitantly. "Last month she said Jonathan was distressed at the home visit as he shared about being pulled off of the football team. Lauren said you explained it was a consequence for lowered schoolwork performance, but she was still concerned this was too harsh of a consequence. While she had me on the phone she asked if we have had any problems with you as foster parents. I told her about earlier this summer when I had met with you and Michael after Jonathan reporting some demeaning language in the heat of an argument."

"That was only one time," I replied. "Did you explain how you came out and talked with us? That we haven't had any other problems?"

"Yes," Tim answered my pleas. "I explained how I met with you both a couple of times. I also told her how we hadn't had any problems before that, and haven't had any since. I have confidence in you adopting the kids, I am not concerned for their safety. I want you to know that, and I told Lauren as well."

"What happened then?" I asked.

"She said she wants to come out tomorrow for a home visit," Tim explained. "She is going to send out an e-mail with the time. I told her I would come too, in case she had any more questions."

"Thanks Tim," I began to feel tears slowly flowing down my face and needed to get off of the phone before Tim could sense it. "I'll see you tomorrow then. Bye."

THE ATTACK

As I hung up the phone I felt as if I couldn't breathe. I called Michael to fill him in and while on the phone with him I couldn't contain my emotions any longer. I got off of the phone quickly and began to sob in the middle of the parking lot. I didn't care if people walked by and saw me. The emotions overflowed in the form of tears and fear and grief came out in moans. This was my greatest fear, something disrupting our process of adoption. *Could this be it? What if Lauren didn't feel like we were fit to be parents?*

I felt like I would vomit in the parking lot and even hunched over in anticipation. I felt light-headed and thankfully caught myself on the van door and sat down in the driver's seat. I rested my head on the steering wheel and sobbed uncontrollably. I turned on some music to try to distract Christina and Kyle who were with me in the van. They remained unusually quiet as I struggled in the front seat.

As the tears slowed down, I noticed I was shaking uncontrollably. My breathing became heavy. I didn't know how I was going to calm down. I needed to go home. Michael was there and I needed him to help reassure me everything was going to be okay. He always seemed so settled in times like these. He was able to keep his thoughts realistic and his emotions in check. I obviously struggled in this area.

As I started to get more control over my breathing I felt like I was finally getting a hold of myself. I drove home, still shaking a little. As I walked in the door Michael tried to talk to me but again my emotions overcame me. He put Christina and Kyle down for a nap and then told me he had called Tim, who was on his way over.

"Why did you call Tim?" I asked, somewhat angry.

"I am worried about you," Michael said boldly, a look of concern on his face.

I didn't want Tim to see me like this. I tried to calm down and push all the feelings down deep in the safety of my heart. Tim arrived and the three of us made small-talked. Then Tim and I went to the backyard to talk.

As Tim asked me what was going on I explained how I was feeling and started to cry again. He tried to help me realize how unlikely my thoughts of losing the kids or having a delayed adoption was. He told me he didn't believe this was so severe it would risk us losing the children. He said he didn't even know if it was going to delay the adoption at all.

"Let's imagine you don't get to adopt this year," he said. "What if you don't adopt the kids until January or even February? What is the worst thing that would happen?"

I thought about the idea for a moment and realized the only thing it affected was my comfort and feelings.

"Every Christmas, for at least the last four years, we thought we'd have kids," I was beginning to get emotional. "It never happened though. Each year my Birthday came on January 4th, reminding me God still hadn't blessed us with children. Now we are hoping to adopt the kids by Christmas and I can't imagine having to wait any longer for it to happen. I can't imagine another calendar year passing without things being official and being able to rest in that knowledge. I need it to happen. I can't wait any more. What if waiting means it might never happen?"

The tears began to flow heavier. I'm not saying it was a logical process, but this was where my mind was. My heart was not only worrying about when we would adopt, but now if we would adopt. Tim tried to help me realize how illogical my thinking was and it did help to talk it out. After we talked, I started to feel better.

"This is easy waiting, this is the happy part," Tim explained. "You are almost to the end. It is disappointing to know you aren't enjoying this time. Instead, you are experiencing a great amount of stress and grief. It might be helpful to meet with someone and talk about it. This isn't how most families react during this time."

I shook my head in agreement as he walked back inside the house.

The next day we had our home visit and Lauren left happy. She planned to submit our paperwork to our adoption attorney within a few days. The visit went well and getting so upset about a possible delay seemed so foolish. It was such an exaggerated reaction to what now seemed so trivial.

In my humanity, I thought everything rested on my shoulders. I assumed a delay would have been my fault. It would have meant I hadn't done something I should have done. In my mind, I would have let everyone down. In these moments it was as if God was teaching me again that He has everything under control and things would happen in His good and perfect timing.

Lauren e-mailed two days later and said she sent all our paperwork to the attorney. The next day, on November 8th, we sat in our attorney's office and signed the adoption petitions. Our attorney told us she normally gets an adoption date when she submits the paperwork but because it was a Friday afternoon and a holiday weekend (Veteran's Day was on the following Monday) we wouldn't get a date until Tuesday when all the necessary people involved could set a date.

That Tuesday morning we got the news that our adoption date was only ten days away and would happen on November 22nd. It seemed surreal in that moment. I remember standing in our entryway and needing to grab the banister of our stairs to keep steady as I heard this amazing news. I hung up the phone with the attorney and called Michael at work to tell him. I was crying, but this time it wasn't tears of fear or sadness. I was in complete awe of how the Lord had everything so perfectly planned again. These were wonderful, happy tears.

MY FIRST THERAPY SESSION

A few days after hearing the news of our adoption date I had my first therapy session. I didn't know what to expect. I had been scared because of my response when hearing of the possible delay in our adoption. This whole process was making me feel utterly unstable. I was an emotional mess, and didn't feel safe. I had never experienced anything like this before. Although, I had been feeling better since we heard the news of our adoption date. Still, overall I felt like a mess and was looking forward to talking about it with someone.

This fostering stage was such an emotional process. I thank God through all my ups and downs he remained constant and unchanging. He never wavered, despite my tendency to become so absorbed in my circumstances and allow what was happening to dictate how I felt.

This first therapy session wasn't necessarily meaningful or impactful. It was nice to talk things through, yet I was currently happy and on cloud nine while we waited for our adoption date to come. I no longer felt at the mercy of my anxiety or fear. I had almost canceled the session because I thought I was better and had just had a "low moment." In actuality, I was again letting my circumstances dictate how I felt. I know now how fleeting all these emotions were.

The therapist and I did a few stress-relieving exercises and I was supposed to practice them several time a days and especially if I felt a heightened level of stress, worry, or fear. As we ended our session she asked when I would like to see her again.

"I'm not sure I'll need to meet again," I told her confidently. "We'll be adopting the kids soon and I think I am just tired of waiting and ready to move on and feel confidence in our family. Then I will feel better and not feel so stressed. It will be a turning point." The therapist was persistent though, and wanted to have another session after the adoption to touch base. If I didn't think it was necessary, I could always cancel, she assured me.

Time went by quickly as we excitedly awaited November 22nd to arrive. Family was coming to visit, friends would gather with us to celebrate over a dinner, and we were even going to be on our local news station to share pieces of our story and promote National Adoption Awareness Month.

As the day got closer, I began to become so emotional, as if I wasn't emotional enough already! If I heard a song that made me extra happy, I would cry. If the kids were being cute, tears. If I took enough time to pause and simply think about how blessed I felt, my face was instantly wet. At least these tears were happy and full of gratitude and awe at our soon-arriving adoption day.

I began to pray for God to give me peace, calmness, and

emotional stability on adoption day. I didn't want to be crying uncontrollably. I wanted to take it all in and enjoy it. I jokingly (but somewhat seriously) told my sister one day, "You want to know where you'll find me at court? I'll be the one sobbing in the corner!"

Adoption Day
Chapter Eleven

I woke up early and as I got Kyle out of bed he looked up at me and said, "Momma!" I hadn't heard him call me "momma" in ten months. During this time we went through many struggles with the children, as you've read, but Kyle not saying "momma" had begun to hurt my heart profoundly.

As I picked him up I cried out, "What did you say big boy?" He said it again, "Momma."

This was the best way to start the day and such a gift to my heart. He hadn't said "momma" in so long and it hurt, yes, but I had even started to be worried he would never say it again. I know, that doesn't make any sense. Yet, that is how my heart felt from the sadness. I hugged Kyle close and tight and tears of love and joy rolled down my face. This was going to be a beautiful day. I was his momma and finally the legal side of things would catch up with how I felt about these children in my heart.

I made breakfast and soon a couple of friends arrived to help do my hair and make-up for the special day ahead. As children started finishing their breakfast they came to my room and I passed out their clothes for court. At one point Jonathan came in and said he had thrown up. I looked over at him as my hair was getting fixed and calmly asked him, "Are you okay? How do you feel now?" He said he actually felt better. I'm guessing his nerves caused the incident. I asked him where the mess was and he said he already cleaned it up and he had just wanted to let me know. Off he went to finish getting ready with a smile.

As he walked away, the ladies doing my hair told me they couldn't believe how calm I had just been when hearing the news that one of my kids had thrown up. I was surprised too! I shared with the ladies how I had been praying all week to have control over my emotions. And I actually felt at peace. I wasn't worried. It seemed like God had answered my prayers for this day. Not only was it here, but I wasn't feeling stressed.

AT THE COURTHOUSE

As we drove to the courthouse we reminded the children exactly what was going to happen. I started talking, "Today is such a special day. Today is the day we officially become a family. We won't have different last names anymore. We will all be *Wells*. Today is the day you will each be made my children forever. No one will be able to take that away." I smiled at them and then continued. "We will be waiting with family and friends in a big waiting area outside of the courtroom until an officer comes out and calls our name. Then we will go inside of the courtroom and sit at a table in front of the judge. All our special guests will get to come inside too, they will sit behind us and watch. The judge will ask daddy and me some questions. Then she will sign the adoption papers and we will be a family forever."

They began asking questions of who would be there exactly and naming people one-by-one asking if they will be there. We didn't know exactly who was going to be coming. We made sure, though, to say the names of those we knew would be there. I listed the names to them, "Ms. Angela, Mr. Tim, Ms. Lauren, Grandma Susie, Grandma Julia, Aunt Andrea, and Alyssa. We know for sure they will be there. Everyone else who comes will be a surprise to all of us!" We went around the car and prayed and thanked God for bringing us together and making us a family.

We walked into the courthouse and the kids were amazed at the big building. We were greeted almost immediately by familiar faces as we waited at the elevators. We arrived at the designated floor and were received by more people who were there to celebrate with us. Joyful people with big smiles celebrating this amazing day with us. More and more family and friends arrived to watch our family be created on paper by the hands of the judge. The news crew arrived and started filming us and asking us how we were feeling. Our photographer was there as well capturing the moments for us to see a visual representation of this day that would never fade away.

We signed all the final paperwork with Lauren, the state adoption worker, and then Michael asked me to stand by the window with him as he talked with me. He told me how excited he was for this day to finally be here. Despite the tears and heartache we had encountered, he praised God who had brought us here, to this day, to this courthouse, where we would become a family. Then he pointed down at the street and told me someone special had just arrived and was walking in now. I look down and saw Maegan quickly crossing the street to come into the courthouse.

Maegan flew from Washington State to Louisville to be here to witness our family being born within the walls of the courtroom. She was the first person I talked to on the phone when I had to interrupt our conversation to switch to the other line. This was a friend who cared for us and prayed for us as well as she could, even though we were separated by more than two thousand miles. She had only seen the children in pictures and on Skype, yet loved and supported us all the same, no matter the distance between us.

I hadn't cried yet that morning except after Kyle called me "momma." In those moments as I waited for Maegan to come up the elevator I started to feel such overwhelming gratitude I could hardly contain the tears. Yet, I breathed deeply and reminded myself I wanted to remain calm and enjoy this day without opening the dam of tears that I was sure wouldn't stop once started.

Maegan came through the elevator and we hugged as she held her newest baby, Kate. Just as we whispered greetings into each other's ears the court officer called out, "All parties on the Wells adoption." Maegan had made it just in time.

I felt my insides trembling as Michael, the kids, and I all sat at the table and awaited the judge's entrance. She walked in and sat down with a friendly greeting. Our adoption attorney began asking us verification questions about the children and ourselves. Then the judge started asking us to confirm our love for the children and if we wanted to adopt them. Michael and I said, "Yes." Yes, we love these children. Yes, we accept them into our family. Yes, we are going to care for them for the rest of our lives. The judge said, "Then it will be as if you had given birth to them." She signed the papers with joy and I could hear Michael wiping away tears and Grandma Susie crying sighs of relief behind us. It was official. Jonathan, Jazmine, Christina, and Kyle belonged to us forever, in our hearts and on paper.

I continued to take deep breaths and hold the tears in. The process, the wait, and the uncertainties were finished. I felt at peace in those first moments around the courthouse table. We adopted the kids. *It really happened.* I was legally their mom.

Pictures continued to be taken and the judge came down to be included in the photos. The news crew kept filming and interviewing reactions to the court proceedings. Soon we realized the judge had another case and we all went back to the waiting area. Our attorney said she was going downstairs to get all the paperwork processed and pressed with the state seal. She said we could meet her down there in about ten minutes.

We went home and the news crew greeted us as we entered the house. More in-depth interviews happened during the next hour as we also ate lunch and started putting the little kids in bed for a nap. That night we gathered again with family and friends (many of which couldn't come to court that morning) over a pizza dinner and with great excitement.

As family and friends gathered around us and congratulated us with hugs and smiles we were resting in the afterglow of the birth of our family. My friend Indy mentioned she was amazed how calm I had been at court and now at dinner.

"I've been thinking about it all day," Indy said. "Then I realized, today was only about the paper trail. In your heart, they've always been your kids."

That night we stayed up to watch the eleven o'clock news and see our segment. My mom, my sister, Michael, Maegan, and I all laughed and smiled as we watched our story (You can watch the segment here: www.bit.ly/from2to6).

Throughout the whole day I was calm. Yet, the first moments of peace after we adopted the kids didn't stay long. After we got up from the table at the courthouse, I felt as if I was watching someone else's life. I was going through the motions. It didn't feel real.

I assumed all the built-up tension and stress and anxiety would release. It did for a moment. But then it didn't go away. It was still there, in the back of my mind, haunting me.

AFTER THE EXCITEMENT WASHED AWAY

Our house was busy all weekend as everyone was still excited from adoption day. I didn't really have time to process through my feelings. Maegan stayed with us through the weekend. It was such a joy to get to spend time with her. As we were preparing on Sunday night for her departure the next day, I shared with her what I thought was going on.

"I don't feel like I was expecting to," I admitted. "All weekend long everything has just felt the same." Maegan replied, "What do you mean?"

"I feel like this is all a dream. Like, it's not real," I said, "I don't know. Maybe all the busyness and excitement is just too much. Right now, though, I just don't feel the peace and confidence I thought I would." Deep down I knew something wasn't right in my heart.

I assumed I would immediately feel an enormous burden lifted from my shoulders. I assumed all the fear and anxiety and stress of the nineteen months of fostering would disappear. The limbo life was over now. The children were ours. Forever. Legal.

That didn't happen though.

"Maybe you'll feel better when you see it, when you get the children's birth certificates in the mail," Maegan said. "Once you don't have home visits anymore, or people constantly checking in. Maybe after a little bit of time it will all feel normal."

I went to bed Sunday night feeling on edge. My emotions were still wild and varied. I thought I would feel confident knowing nothing was going to happen to the kids and they were ours, legally. Yet, I still felt like something was going to fall through and someone was going to come to our house and say the adoption didn't really count and we weren't really their parents.

Maegan left Monday morning and life was back to normal. Yet deep down, I was still anxious and fearful.

CONTINUED THERAPY

"Why do you still need to see the therapist?" Michael asked me. The truth was I had only told Maegan how I was feeling. I left Michael and everyone else I knew in the dark. I didn't want to talk about it. I felt ashamed and embarrassed. I should be happy and relieved and living life. Yet I was still feeling as if I was living with a dark cloud over me.

"How are you?" The therapist asked as she sat down in our living room.

I started crying as I opened up about how I didn't feel right. I hadn't had the emotional reaction at court, or after. I had felt like much of the day I was witnessing the events instead of living them. I then told her it didn't feel real. I was still feeling like something was going to happen and things weren't guaranteed or safe. I told her I didn't feel like I could rest, I didn't feel at peace.

She spoke comforting words as she told me how she believes the after-adoption care of foster parents is one of the most lacking resources in this process.

"How do people expect foster parents to be on edge and many times full of anxiety in the process and then it just suddenly lifted because you have papers in your hand that say the kids are yours?" she asked.

It was a relief to know there wasn't something wrong with me. I was so worried with the anxiety attack and now this that I had some unstable emotional or mental condition. I wondered why I was feeling so many extreme and adverse reactions throughout this process.

As we talked through therapy I realized she was right. I carried the weight of foster care for nineteen months thinking constantly that everything rested on me to be sure things were continually moving along. *How was I supposed to just turn the switch off now that things were settled and final?*

The therapist and I went on to explore where this control problem had stemmed from. For the first time I began to realize why I constantly had to make sure everything happened right, or else take the guilt of failure upon myself. As a child my parents worked long hours. At times I felt like my world was out of control and unbalanced. We had financial struggles, my parents fought all the time, and I just wanted to feel like a kid. I often tried to do what I could to keep the peace and make sure my sister was taken care of. I learned it was safest to count on myself and strive to do what needed done so I wouldn't be yelled at. I struggled to trust others and relinquish control outside of my own hands.

Additionally, Michael and I had experienced so much disappointment on our way to parenthood and, deep down, I was worried this was going to eventually end up just another disappointment. Why after all these years of struggling should I rest in confidence that this happy ending was real and long-lasting?

At the end of the session the therapist spoke confirming words to my heart. She reminded me of great truths, "You are your children's mother. It is done. It is over. It is final. They are yours. No one is going to take that away." She also told me to say those truths out loud throughout the day and especially at times when I felt the worry and fear were rising within me.

Life Goes On
Chapter Twelve

I continued to see the therapist for a month following our adoption. We had two to three sessions a week and worked hard to talk through my feelings and also do stress-relieving exercises to help me calm down when moments of anxiety attacked.

I was starting to feel better as therapy went on. We did receive the children's new birth certificates, with Michael and my name printed on the line for the parents. It was surreal to hold those papers in my hands. Plus life just went on, as it always does. We were homeschooling the kids now and enjoying being with them at home more. Christmas approached and we were excited to take a trip to Ohio to see extended family for the first time since adoption day.

I still hadn't told anyone else how I was feeling, or why I was still seeing the therapist. Other than Maegan, my friends didn't even know I was seeing a therapist. Despite the progress I had seen since adoption day, I still felt quite ashamed of having struggled in this way. I wanted to be a mother for so long and now had four children. Why couldn't I be happy and enjoy life more without the constant fear something was going to go wrong?

During one of the therapy sessions I mentioned I hadn't told anyone except Maegan about what I was going through. The therapist asked me if I felt confident enough to tell Michael, and then maybe share it with a few friends before our next session. I said yes, although I wasn't quite sure. I was ready to move on though, and I thought telling more people would help me do that. We practiced how I was going to share the news during that session until I felt comfortable with the words coming out of my mouth.

I waited for a good time to talk to Michael and then just said it. We were lying in bed one night and his arm was wrapped around me. I said, "I want to tell you about why I'm still seeing the therapist. I'm not looking for an answer, or for you to fix anything. I just want you to listen and hear what's going on." He said okay and I just laid it out there. He tightened his embrace and kissed my head. He whispered, "You don't have to worry any more. It's done. We did it. They're ours."

The next day I told my sister, who replied saying this was typical me, always carrying the weight of the world. As I started telling people I began to feel the weight of shame lifted off of me.

A few days later I attended my monthly book club and while everyone was greeting each other and grabbing snacks a friend noticed me and asked, "I haven't seen you since adoption day. How are things going? Do you finally feel relief from the pressure of everything?"

I paused for a moment and thought about how I wanted to answer the questions. *Did I want to pretend like everything was great? Or did I trust this group enough to be honest and vulnerable?* I chose the latter. I shared with her, and the rest of the room became quiet as I started talking. I said, "Adoption day was great. However, I haven't been feeling relief. I have still been struggling, all the more, since adoption day with the fear that something is still going to fall through. But I have been seeing a therapist and working through the feelings. Not only that, but I am finally starting to feel like life is normal and everything is going to be okay."

I don't think anyone expected me to speak so honestly. Most of the time, even in the midst of struggles, we are so quick to say we are doing just fine even though at times it feels like the world is falling from under us. This group of women accepted me despite my shortcomings and struggles. I wasn't ridiculed or chastised. I was accepted and welcomed.

As long as I held the truth of my feelings inside, I wasn't going to get better. It was only when I shared the hard and ugly truth with those closest to me I began to see a change in my heart. I believe this is part of why God designed us to live in community with one another. We aren't meant to bear our burdens alone.

First, God wants us to cast our cares on him (1 Peter 5:7). Second, we are not meant to live on this earth in isolation. We have to take the risk of opening ourselves up to others and being vulnerable. In doing this, we experience life together. That's how it's meant to be lived. Our struggles only grow stronger in the dark, we must bring them into the light and own it for what it really is. Then we can truly begin to move on.

BURNT-OUT ON LIFE

My next therapy session would be my last and during it I committed to my therapist I was going to work hard at taking care of myself and not holding the weight and burden of responsibility when it wasn't mine to carry.

In the following weeks after the burden of fear began to be lifted, I realized how burnt-out I was on life and how utterly exhausted I was. I had been so worried about the children and caring for all of their needs and getting to adoption day I never realized the cost of my continual stress, worry, and lack of self-care. I had been giving of myself for nineteen months. I was worn out.

I think I experienced something like an adrenaline rush, similar to when you are in a car accident. You are handling details with your car and you may feel fine in the moment. Yet, when you get home and start to relax you realize you are in serious pain. Maybe I was running on adrenaline for nineteen months and now I was realizing how I felt when the stress and fear and worry were starting to fade. It was not good. I had been surviving for so long I didn't even know what it meant to thrive and actually live.

Life had become more like a burden to carry rather than a gift of grace to enjoy each day. I didn't want to live as a bystander to my own life. I only get one chance at this. I want to thrive. I want to be all there and all in for the sake of God and those I love dearly.

I spent the next couple of months getting back into a good sleep routine, reading more for enjoyment and stress relief, and taking time away to refuel my mind, body, and spirit. I started to feel like me again. And feeling like me again made me a better wife, mother, and friend.

THE BLESSED CHAOS

This year, 2014, has been a great year for our family. It is definitely the beginning of the rest of our lives. We are taking all the heartache and tears and struggles of what our life has been and are moving forward together. We started the year as a family.

This year together has added so much comfort and security into our hearts. The children are thriving in our home and in their place in our family. I cannot believe how quickly time goes by. When this book comes out we will be celebrating our one-year adoption anniversary.

Yet, life is not perfect. Adoption wasn't a quick fix to all of our problems. Everything our children have been through still affects them regularly. Everything I've been through still affects me. But we know we are in this together. Michael and I are committed to these children for life, no matter what happens. They are ours. We all take confidence in that proclamation.

This was all part of our story and part of God's plan. I know now He redeemed every tear and made it worth it. The bad days, struggles, and chaos are nothing compared to the overwhelming blessedness of our life with these children.

As I stood in church during July of this year (2014), surrounded by Michael and the kids, we were singing *Your Love Never Fails*. As the song continued on we were repeating the line, *"In all things, You work for my good"*[11]. I couldn't hold back the joyful overwhelming tears as I raised my hands high. I knew those words to be true. Standing next to me as proof, my four children. Everything we went through was worth it and it led to this point: My life is blessed chaos. I GET to be their mom. I wouldn't have it any other way.

---

[11] This line is altered from the original song by our worship pastor.

God took my brokenness and their brokenness and brought us together to create beauty, right in the middle of it all. Our family was not an afterthought, it was God's plan. Jonathan says God did all of this to bring us together. I believe it too.

Earlier this summer Jonathan came to me after processing what spiritual adoption meant and said, "I think about how my life used to be and how everything changed, and I just know. How can God NOT be real? He took me from all the bad and brought me to a family that loves me. He changed my life. I will never be the same. He saved me."

Why? Why did God bring them to me? Not just for my happiness or the kid's well-being, while those blessings are part of the outcome. The ultimate reason God did all of this was for His glory and the furthering of His Kingdom. He is using our story to tell people about Himself. When you read the intimate details of it all you can't help but see His hand in the midst of it. May I never grow tired of sharing the brokenness and the beauty of how God brought life into my home and the once-empty places of my life.

Afterword

I asked Jonathan one night after the other three children were in bed if he would share about his adoption journey. He dictated what he wanted me to type for you to read. At some points when Jonathan was talking, he didn't know what to say. Therefore, at times I prompted him with questions. My questions are found in parentheses.

(Do you remember the day you first met us?) I remember the day I first met my mom and dad. I was so shy. It took me a while to get used to calling my mom "Mom" instead of Ms. Ashley. It was hard to call Mr. Michael my dad too. (What made it hard?) Knowing they aren't my biological parents and that I have other parents living somewhere else was hard. (What makes it easy now?) I'm adopted and there is no going back. This is my life now, they are my parents now.

After a while, everything settled down and I got used to this new life. I have a new mom and dad and they play with me. I like how we hang out together and spend time together. They love me very much. My new mom and dad don't spend their money on drugs or other stuff, they spend it on me.

I also love how I never go hungry. I'm always stuffed full and can pig out if I want to. We would go days sometimes without food at my old house because my biological parents would spend their money on drugs. When they did buy us food, it wasn't very healthy. It didn't help me grow stronger.

I'm glad that my parents now love me and they go places with me and want to be around me. We eat dinner together every day with people that love each other. We love to just be together as a family.

What I like most about being with my new parents is being able to take pictures together to show our love for each other. Things like spending Christmas together and having mud fights with my Aunt Andrea.

When I got adopted I felt amazing because then I knew my old life was gone and I didn't have to look back anymore. I can just look at the future and know that everything is okay. No one is going to break into our house, or come at me with a gun. No one is going to take me away. I'm safe now. When it was adoption day I felt so happy and I just wanted to cry. I saw my dad crying and it made me amazingly happy to know how loved I was.

(What was the hardest part of being in foster care?) It was hard because I felt like my new parents might not love me because I would get in trouble a lot. (Has that fear changed?) Yes, I know that my mom and dad will never stop loving me, just like God, no matter what I do. Their love doesn't change if I am in trouble. They want to teach me what is right and wrong and help me to grow up to be a Godly man who takes care of his family.

When I came here is when I started to learn about God. At my old house, I didn't know about God. I just thought we had to try our best and live and then die. Now I know that there is a God and if you believe in Him you don't just live and die. When you die you get to spend eternity with God. He is everything. I want to live for Him. And He never stops loving me.

Back then, I had a cat and I would throw it around and kick it. But now I have three cats and love them and feed them and even sleep with them if they come up on my bed. (What does that say about how you have changed?) I have learned so much more about loving people and not being angry. It has changed me. I am a different person and I can love others and animals.

Also back then I would get into a lot of fights. I would come home with bloody noses or with bruises from beating someone up. But now I am strong and try to treat others with kindness and respect.

(What is the one thing that you learned most through your adoption journey?) What I've learned most is that there is a

God and He loves us and He gave me new parents because he knew that I wasn't safe at my old house. He knew that my new family and house was better for me, so He brought me here. He saved me.

Resources

In writing this book, I knew I wanted to offer more than just our story. I wanted to give you some resources I wish I had when going through our journey.

To best serve you, I have created an online page with resources:

www.bit.ly/BlessedChaosResources

Wherever you are on your journey, you will find resources on this page to help!

Acknowledgements

God is first and foremost responsible for the journey. My journey started with the brokenness of infertility and ends in a beautiful story of motherhood and blessed chaos every day with four children in my home. It was His glorious amazing plan and He orchestrated every step along the way.

To Michael, you are such an important person in my life and in this story. It is a joy and honor to be your wife. You were so brave to trust my heart when I felt God leading us to adopt through foster care. You led and continue to lead our family. Most importantly, you prayed for our future and trusted the Lord's guiding even when I was not certain. I wouldn't have wanted to take this journey with anyone else but you! Not only that, but this book wouldn't have been possible had it not been for you giving me the time it took to write it out. I will forever be thankful for that gift.

Jonathan, Jazmine, Christina, and Kyle, you have filled my home with so much joy and laughter and love. It is truly a privilege to be your mother. I know the Lord chose you to be my sons and daughters. You are each amazing and a special gift to me! I will do my best to cherish you every day and remember always that my being your mother has come at a great cost.

To my kids' birthparents, this story would not have come to be had the life of these four children been casted aside. Thank you for choosing life for these precious souls. Their lives are a gift that you give to me again and again every day.

Flourish Bloggers (Kristin, Jennifer, Beth, Lori and Victoria), thank you for walking with me through this journey. Thank you ladies for being there, supporting me, and for helping me make this book the best it could be! Jennifer and Kristin, you especially supported me by offering your help and encouragement along the way.

Maegan and Jo, your friendships are invaluable to me. I cannot begin to count the times you've listened to me talk about this book, or the ways you have helped and cheered me on.

Becky, you are the first person I heard the term *blessed chaos* from. Thank you! What a perfect picture of how life is.

Thank you to the many people who supported us locally and around the globe through prayer, blog comments, e-mails, Facebook messages, meals, listening ears, and so much more! You will never truly understand how much you encouraged me throughout this journey!

About the Author

Ashley Wells is a proud wife and mother to four. She is a writer, speaker, self-publishing fan, and sweet tea addict. She is particularly passionate about living intentionally as a Christian woman, being inspired daily as a mother, and using her journey through foster care and adoption to ignite a fire in the hearts of others to care for orphans. Ashley also loves to help women realize they have a message to share and their words, whether written or spoken, can impact the lives of others.

Above all, though, Ashley's heart beats most strongly to reach women right where they are and remind them they are not alone in this life.

To connect with Ashley, visit her website at www.ashleykwells.com.

Printed in Great Britain
by Amazon